An Introduction To Philosophy In Education

An Introduction To Philosophy In Education

William G. Samuelson
Fred A. Markowitz

Emporia State University

Philosophical Library
New York

Library of Congress Cataloging-in-Publication Data

Samuelson, William G., 1938-
　An introduction to philosophy in education.

　Bibliography: p.
　1. Education—United States—Philosophy—History.
2. Idealism.　3. Realism.　4. Pragmatism.　5. Existentialism.　I. Markowitz, Fred A., 1924- 　. II. Title.
LA212.S25　　　　1987　　　　370'.1　　　　87-14067
ISBN 0-8022-2541-1
Copyright 1988 by Philosophical Library, Inc.
200 West 57 Street, New York, N.Y. 10019
Manufactured in the United States of America

Table of Contents

8 An Introduction To Philosophy In Education

Preface

This book is an introduction to the study of philosophy and its application to education. It is addressed principally to upper division undergraduate students in professional education and graduate students in their first course in foundations or philosophy of education. More advanced students may also find the book's organization and content to be a new and useful approach to the study of both philosophy and education.

Four philosophies which have had a great impact on the development of American education are idealism, realism, pragmatism, and existentialism. What these four philosophies mean as theories and how they impinge on education is the subject of this book. While a case might be made for including other philosophies (or other labels), such coverage is outside the scope of this volume. (One should consider, too, that other philosophies—such as neo-Thomism, experimentalism, and empiricism—are often hybrids or logical developments of the basic four philosophies highlighted in this work.)

In the first section of the book, each of the four philosophies is defined in relation to concepts such as truth, value, freedom, love, culture, power, change. In the second section the philosophies are applied to educational issues and topics, for example, curriculum, learning, the teacher's role, discipline, individual pupil differences, school buildings and budgets, and school climate.

The reader will note that, under each topic, idealism is explained first, then realism, pragmatism, and existentialism. The four philosophies are presented in this sequence to indicate the order of their historical appearance and their impact on American life and schools. The reader could develop the impression that idealism suffers from being presented first under each topic; however, idealism was the first philosophy to influence educational thought and practice. The subsequent appearance of other educational philosophies grew as communication among people and nations expanded, beliefs changed, and society developed.

This book contains neither recommended readings nor primary source material, although serious students will, no doubt, turn to sources listed in the bibliography or other references to pursue more deeply their particular philosophical interests. The singular aim in these pages is to provide a simplified overview of philosophy in education that will be of help to students as they are being introduced to the subject and as they become engaged in educational practice. Such an overview exists nowhere else.

Section I

Philosophies and Topics

In order to comprehend the modern American school it is necessary to understand the four basic philosophies that have contributed to its development. These philosophies are idealism, realism, pragmatism, and existentialism. Without such understanding, students may find themselves bewildered by, and unaware of, what gave rise to the abundant variety of educational goals and objectives, curricular elements, and instructional methods that characterize contemporary American education.

At the present time there are probably no schools which are controlled by only one philosophy, although one might find some schools which are heavily influenced by only one or two. Teachers, too, are likely to be influenced by more than one philosophy. To understand what is going on in schools and why it is happening it is helpful to know the historical and philosophical origins of these practices.

In idealism one sees a philosophy which is ancient yet contemporary. In its most recognizable form it is seen in churches but it is also reflected in nationalism and patriotism. It has its roots in beliefs and faith in forces greater than the individual—God, Jehovah, Allah, or often, kings, emperors, and one-party governments. In this volume these superior forces are collectively referred to as "super force."

Realism, which has emerged in the last five hundred years, is typified by those who want to take the most objective, careful, and scientific look at the world. Such people believe that nature in its order and symmetry is the source of all of the knowledge that humans need. If human beings will only use the tools of science and logic appropriately, they can learn everything that they need to know to live in societal harmony.

The pragmatist, on the other hand, expresses some positive regard for science and its methods but does not believe in fixed or unchanging truths as both the idealist and realist are prone to do. The pragmatist is basically a practical person who wants to know costs and consequences. Pragmatists believe they should be constantly at work reorganizing and structuring their environment to achieve more socially useful outcomes.

The existentialist influence can be seen in the lives and actions of those people who believe in placing a high value on individual choice and personal freedom, who profess that one should live life fully and authentically. They resist conforming to externally imposed or inherited standards. They consider the development of their own potential as paramount. They emphasize choice-making in the light of both alternatives and consequences.

All four of these philosophies can be seen at work in the typical American public school. The degree to which they are represented and the fervor with which they are advocated will determine how a given school is conducted. These philosophies and their logical extensions (or hybrids), such as neo-Thomism, empiricism, or classical realism, have had a tremendous shaping effect on the structure of contemporary American education.

Some liberties have been taken in the presentation of the four philosophies in order to draw clear lines of distinction between them for the beginner. For example, idealism is presented here in a rather traditional and fundamental form. It is not neo-Thomism with its integration of realistic thought, but rather a less complicated (perhaps "purer") form of idealism. It should be recognized that many contemporary idealists are also influenced by other philosophies and may not be as intractable as presented here.

Realism is presented as a philosophy owing a primary debt to nature and science. Realism in this model is uninfluenced by other philosophies.

Pragmatism as it is presented demonstrates a rejection of all absolutes but two: a belief in relativity and in democratic social processes.

Existentialism is offered as a non-theistic or non-religious philosophy in order to draw the clearest lines of distinction between it and idealism. It should be noted, however, that there are many religious existentialists.

Truth

Idealism

For the idealist truth exists. It exists apart from human experience. It is truth with a capital T—absolute, eternal, and universal. The truth is known perfectly only to super force. Humans discover truths which are already existent, or truths are revealed to them either by super force, by the authorities or interpreters of super force, or by reading the collected wisdom and discoveries already made by those great thinkers and prophets who have gone before us. Whether one believes that truth is innate (already existing within the individual at birth and waiting to be drawn out or brought to consciousness by teachers or parents) or one believes that truth exists in the mind of super force or some "place," such as Plato's world of ideas or Hegel's cycle of history, the idealist believes that truth is mental or spiritual in nature. The use of prayer, reflection or meditation, inductive thinking or Aristotelian logic, revelation, and significant books and writings, as well as authorities and interpreters of super force, will all lead one to discover the *truth*.

Realism

For the realist truth exists. It may be known imperfectly or perfectly by humans depending upon their skill and advancement. Truth exists in nature and in the laws that govern the interaction of the elements of nature. Humans can discover these existing laws through accurate observation, the use of scientific principles, and the application of deductive reasoning. The truth as it exists in nature is absolute and eternal and universal. Realists approach truth like the explorer or the investigative scientist; they observe carefully, gather data, and apply the method of science to find the truth. Scientist realists are continuously testing and trying to verify and document their hypothetical truths in their search for the truths of nature.

Pragmatism

For the pragmatist truth is a function of the interaction of the human intellect and the environment. This simultaneous mutual interaction, commonly called by pragmatists the reconstruction or reconstitution of experience, creates or invents truth. The pragmatist is a relativist where truth is concerned, for he or she sees it as changeable and dependent on the experiences of the perceiver and the environment in which it is experienced. The pragmatist believes that there are no absolutes and that change is the only constant. Truth exists only as a function of the human mind which uses social experience, scientific methods, and personal reflection or insight in the process of reconstructing or reconstituting experience to give it more improved social impact. For the pragmatist, whether a thing is true or not is probably not as important as whether it has practical and useful applications which are good for both the individual and social environment in which one operates.

Existentialism

For the existentialist truth is a matter of personal interpretation and choice. Truth is not absolute because it is determined by humans based upon their individual concepts of personal relevance, or the meanings that things have for them, or the meanings which they attach to the events in their world. Truth is personally relative; it is a matter of choosing and then acting on one's choices. For the existentialist, then, truth requires choice making, personal action, and acceptance by the individual of the real life consequences of one's actions. Truth, choice, responsibility, and action go hand in hand. "The truth is that for which I will act." It is also that which the individual judges will lead to personal "authenticity."

Value

Idealism

For the idealist, value, like truth, exists apart from human activity. Value is closely related to the concept of truth for the idealist. The values in idealism are manifestations of truth. Value (or values) come from super force. Those values do not change over time because the truths to which they relate do not change. Values are good from one generation to another. They explicitly and implicitly provide the model for how one ought to act (as super force would have humans act). All values have already been discovered and written down in sacred or holy books, or in revered political documents, or recorded other places in the library and in the minds of the wise men or the ancients. Humans find out about values the same way that they learn about truths (by discovery or revelation).

Realism

Value for the realist exists apart from human activity. Values can be discovered by careful and accurate observations of nature and of humans in society (human society being as much a part of nature as a beehive or an ant colony). The social scientist confirms the values inherent in nature, which are actually the laws which govern nature revealed to human understanding by application of careful scientific methodology. The realist who is a social scientist rejects the idea of values coming from something like super force and is careful not to think of nature in terms of "Mother Nature" or any other personification or deification of nature into anthropomorphic forms. The social scientist relies upon testing and measurement as tools for observing humans en masse and uses normative data returns of such observation to determine (reveal) the values implicit in nature and in human social environments.

Pragmatism

To the pragmatist the idea of looking to super force or to the laws of nature to find values is not acceptable. The pragmatist sees the determination of value as a function of social human interaction. Humans create values by their actions and the consequences of their actions. The pragmatist is concerned with questions such as "Are they practical or useful, and do they have positive consequences for individuals and for the larger social referent group?" For the pragmatist, values, like truth, arise from the use of human intellect interacting with the social environment. One value or concept to which the pragmatist is committed is the concept of democracy and the democratic political process. Such a process is based upon belief in the basic equality and rights of individuals in society.

Existentialism

The existentialist sees value as the natural function of individual choice and action. It is also personally relevant and emotive. Each person creates his or her own values through choosing and acting. The existentialist sees values as being individually relative. What is to be considered valuable is that which moves one toward being an authentic being and which enhances one's personhood and one's freedom. "Choose as you would have all humans choose." Through choices one gives license to all others to choose freely, thereby creating a kind of social morality or social contract.

Nature of the Human Being

Idealism

To the idealist, human beings are viewed as the creation and as the servant of super force. The human being is seen as super force's highest creation. Humans are spiritual and mental beings who are part of super force's grand plan. They are subject to the will of super force and are basically passive. Idealists have a tendency to want to define human beings by listing their characteristics or essences, that is, good, bad, evil, spiritual. Idealists tend to see humans as either good or bad by nature, and most Western religiously-oriented idealists tend to see humans as bad or evil until saved or cleansed. Many idealists, though not all, believe in innate knowledge (that humans are born with the knowledge of good and evil and other knowledge already in their minds but not at a conscious level). Idealists tend to view children as miniature adults and hold them accountable as such for misbehavior. Because idealists view humans as basically bad, they tend to view children as beings that have to be made to do right "lest bad habits get rewarded" (as the twig is bent so the tree is inclined). Childhood is often seen as a time of struggle. With the coming of the age of accountability, the child is dealt with as an adult and not as a minor. Human beings are believed to be improvable but not perfectible because only super force is perfect.

Realism

Human beings are viewed by realists as the beings at the top of the evolutionary ladder and as nature's highest product to date. Humans are therefore creatures of nature and part of the natural order of things. Human beings are rational animals who are subject to the laws of nature. Humans are seen not as active or passive but rather as reactive. They are stimulated by events and they react. The human mind is viewed by most of them as some sort of empty or undeveloped entity into which experience is poured or added or as a blank slate upon which experience is recorded. The realist is likely to proclaim that "we are the sum total of our experiences." Children are seen as little creatures (animals) which must be domesticated. They are seen as being naturally good but untaught. Society has the capacity to maintain that natural goodness or to teach (deliberately or accidentally) habits which are bad. Society, therefore, is viewed as a potential corruptor. From their extensive study of children realists possess a tendency to think of childhood somewhat clinically as a series of stages through which children must pass to reach adulthood. Sometimes these may be viewed as stages of child development about which no one can do much, and so adults must simply endure them until the children are old enough to talk to as adults and exercise adult reason.

Pragmatism

Human beings are looked upon by pragmatists as individuals living in societies. The pragmatists would describe human beings as biological, social, and psychological organisms in which those three functions are continuously interacting. The human being is viewed as being interactive with its environment (simultaneously mutually interactive). The human is a learning, experiencing, adapting, and adopting organism. The pragmatists take a somewhat different view of children—seeing them as social individuals who have problems now and lives in progress. They are participants in life. Where the human mind is concerned, the pragmatist says that the mind experiences the environment and that the new experiences are recorded along with the old. In the mind the experiences interact with each other and there is a continuous condition of restructuring or reconstructing or reconstituting of experience. The human being is seen as basically neutral with the capacity to learn to be good or bad, as defined by society. The pragmatist also believes that what is learned can be unlearned.

Existentialism

Existentialists see humanity in a somewhat different perspective. Human beings are seen as potential in motion and in the process of defining themselves through their choices and their actions (being or becoming). They are seen as rational and irrational, as absurd or pathetic, and as authentic. Human beings attach meaning and they personalize everything which has meaning to them. Human beings are viewed as being transactional internally and socially (influencing and being influenced). Children may not have had their existential moment (their realization of alienation and aloneness and their realization of selfhood); nevertheless, they are choosing selves who need practice and assistance choosing and understanding the consequences of their choices. They have the potential to become authentic selves or to become conforming inauthentic "phonies." The labels of good or bad are societal labels and as such have little meaning to the existentialist. The human being is (exists). The key sentence in existentialism is "I am!" This means that one is a thinking, feeling, choosing being who is responsible for the consequences of one's choices and actions. Beyond that the existentialist lists neither characteristics nor essences because to do so is to predefine the potential in each of us. The greatest loss is the loss of human potential and the surrendering of freedom.

The Good Life

Idealism

The good life to the idealist is found in spiritual and mental harmony with super force. The individual believes that life should be lived according to super force's grand plan incorporating the virtues of the prevailing idealist culture. The good life is defined by pursuing excellence and academics and living the life of sacrifice and service to forces greater than the individual. The good life is spiritual and mental; it involves development of the intellectual and the spiritual elements. The epitome is a life of scholarship, service, and sacrifice in harmony with super force and the absolutes.

Realism

For the realist the good life can be achieved by humans who can reach a state of harmony with nature and the natural and physical laws of the universe. The individual should conform to the laws of nature and not be destructive of nature but work in concert with it in science, social endeavors, ecology. The life in harmony with nature is achieved by understanding, being an accurate observer, using higher mental processes (including scientific methods and deductive reasoning). The realist perceives the good life as basically mental with the fullest possible development of the intellect. A life of scholarship, science, and astute observation are required to achieve harmony with nature and its laws. Knowledge is power.

Pragmatism

When the pragmatist speaks of the good life, it is a condition in which the individual is in mutual harmony with self and the society. This is a delicate balance requiring constant alertness. It is defined as being socially and politically active, serving one's fellow human beings and society, and committing one's self to democratic principles and processes. Furthermore, the good life is one of useful, practical, social, and political action in which one strives to develop selfhood and contribute to society. It contains elements of individual achievement and group successes. The rights of all are protected through democratic processes, and the individual is in harmony (as an individual) with society.

Existentialism

The good life to an existentialist is the very important matter of achieving one's potential and choosing to become an authentic being. The individual chooses and acts in authentic ways. The good life is one in which the individual self is most fully and authentically developed. There are aesthetic, emotive, intellectual, and spiritual aspects to be developed in the free expression of the nonconformist authentic self. A state of being is achieved and there is harmony with the self as life is examined fully and carefully. Actions are congruent with the emerging self.

Tradition

Idealism

For idealists the proper role of tradition is to provide structure and meaning to lives that may be empty without it. Tradition structures society and provides a safe anchor to the past. History and the past are very important to idealists. The ancients, their wisdom and writings, are often venerated. Traditions form a body of almost unwritten law, so powerful are they. Heroes and heroines as models from the past are respected and portrayed in contemporary life. The origins of most significant traditions are lodged in antiquity and are based in super force.

Realism

Initially realists rejected the weight of idealist traditions, largely because they (realists) reject super forces and the total acceptance of "wisdom from the past." Gradually, over the years, realists have developed some traditions and heroes and heroines of their own which are rooted largely in science and nature. The realist continues to question or reject idealist traditions as well as those of realism.

Pragmatism

Pragmatists have no use for total acceptance of traditions or practices that promote conformity to the past. They reject tradition and expect that all traditions and rituals and values should be re-examined and tested to determine their practicability and utility in a contemporary setting. There is also a concern for those actions which violate democratic social structure and promote one group or class at another's expense. Traditions per se have no meaning aside from the use which can be made of them. Pragmatists may recognize some heroes and heroines of democracy but will treat them differently from the way they would be treated by an idealist.

Existentialism

Because the existentialist holds the individual self to be more important than socially-oriented tradition or culture, it is understandable that existentialists are individuals who have nothing to do with close conformity to tradition. They believe that the exercise of freedom and the development of personhood will be hindered by unquestioned acceptance of tradition.

Freedom

Idealism

Freedom to the idealist is a somewhat paradoxical concept of individual freedom exercised only within the limits which are set by super force and tradition. Conformity to an ideal and the freedom that comes from conforming to that ideal exemplify the concept. Idealists see human beings as subordinate to the will of super force. Different types of idealism hold differing views on the issue of free will. Although most accept the aforementioned concept of freedom within limits, the more fundamental forms of idealism tend to reject the notion of free will altogether.

Realism

The most reasonable definition of freedom for realists is the exercise of free choice within the limitations set by nature and natural law. Whereas the idealists might have said, "If God meant for man to fly, he would have been born with wings!" the realist is more likely to say, "How can we use what we know of nature's laws to overcome the problem presented by man's weight/mass/power differential which keeps him from flying as a bird does?" Where social and personal freedom are concerned, the realist regards humans as possessing the freedom to operate within the norms and laws of society. Human beings are rational animals who are subordinate to the laws of nature; yet humans are also seen as the victims or products of genetics and environment (nature and nurture). Free will (if such a thing exists for human beings) would be dependent on all of nature's forces at work on (and in) a human being at the instance of choosing.

Pragmatism

The pragmatist views freedom as the capacity to think and create within a social-political context of democracy and doing what is legal, reasonable, and good for the individual and growth of society. This sets some of the same sorts of limits as might be found in idealism and realism; however, the pragmatist's acceptance of relativism and change would seem to permit broader definitions and wider limits of freedom. The individual is encouraged to develop personally and thereby contribute to an improved society. The democratic ideal of freedom with individual acceptance of responsibility is paramount. Free will is an acceptable notion to pragmatists who give it a responsible social "twist."

Existentialism

The existentialist knows (believes) that humans exist. The most important sentence for the existentialist is "I am!" Human beings individually are free to develop or create themselves and to give meaning to their existence. Existentialists come closest of the four to the concept of total freedom primarily because of their basic concern for mental, spiritual, intellectual freedom. They accept the concept of free will as long as one accepts the consequences of one's actions. Says the existentialist, "I am my freedom, I am!"

Creativity

Idealism

To the idealist super force is understood to be the creator of all things. Creativity is a gift from super force to human beings. Some humans receive the gift and some do not. Ultimately, all of human creative efforts should glorify super force and portray appropriate human action, that is, denial of self, sacrifice, service, reverence, martyrdom. Religious and nationalistic themes are often sharply reflected in idealist artistic works. The critic's role as the judge of what is good, beautiful, ugly, or unacceptable is a very important function in the creative enterprise, for the critic represents tradition.

Realism

For the realist creativity is a genetic gift of nature and must be nurtured in proper environments to be developed. Nature is the creator through natural selection and the evolutionary process. Creative efforts in the fine arts which are most valued by realists are those which imitate and portray nature in its unspoiled simplicity. Emphasis on mastering the many elements of technique and almost photographic realism are the keys. Critics are very concerned with mastery of technique and imitation of life. What happens in the laboratory or the science hall is not viewed as creative but rather as a process of discovery of relationships and laws which exist but are unknown. The artist, musician, and poet must also discover laws and relationships in order to successfully and realistically portray the artistic subject.

Pragmatism

The pragmatist believes that humans use their minds as instruments to create knowledge and truth; therefore, they see invention and creation as the result of reflecting (consciously or non-consciously) on human experiences. There is always an environmental context to pragmatist creation because humans exist in several environments simultaneously (social, biological, emotional) and are mutually interactive with all of them on a continuous basis. As far as products or processes are concerned, the pragmatist is probably more interested in invention (practicality) than in creativity (aesthetics). Art forms will tend to focus on themes such as progress, evolution, and social group interaction.

Existentialism

The creation and attachment of meaning and personal relevance as one strives to become an authentic being is the epitome of creativity to the existentialist. The most significant creation is the development of one's authenticity—overcoming alienation, anguish, despair, and dread. In the fine arts there are two dominant artistic themes. The first is a portrayal of human absurdity and stupidity as human beings live conforming, inauthentic lives. The second is the tendency toward abstract or other non-traditional art forms of personal relevance to the artist. The individual and his or her perceptions and meanings are more important than what meanings or labels others may attach to these productions; therefore, a critic's role is unimportant.

Power

Idealism

Super force is the idealist's source of all things, power included. Super force is the supreme power. Power comes from super force. The fundamental idealist tends to believe in social theories that state explicitly or implicitly that super force has invested some classes, nations, or families with more power than others (the "chosen people"). What power humans have should be used for good and to protect "our way of life," as well as to glorify super force.

Realism

For the realist power is a natural function of relationships in nature. The realist scientist talks easily of the release of energy, or of the acquisition of wealth, or the development of knowledge as power. Nature is powerful, and humans achieve power by learning to harness and utilize the laws and powers of nature. Growing out of the development of the intellectual and rational thinking processes (education, logic, deduction, science, knowledge) humans can do a better job of harmonizing with nature and will have more power to use.

Pragmatism

The pragmatist understands power to be the result of human interaction (between individuals) in social environments. The individual has power inherently and surrenders it to others for joint social or political action. In like manner, the individual may become more powerful than others by the powers given to him by others whether willingly, through trickery, or by coercion. Power should be used for the benefit of individuals who will, in turn, improve society.

Existentialism

Like the pragmatist, the existentialist believes that human beings have power, but goes further to state that they have power over their own lives, thoughts, feelings, choices, and actions and are also totally responsible for how they use that power. Power should be used to fulfill one's potential and to achieve authenticity. Power cannot be given away (as pragmatists might view it) because one is always responsible and must always accept the consequences of one's action or choices.

Morality

Idealism

Moral principles and ethical behavior are dependent for idealists upon super force and the laws, traditions, and ideals founded in super force. Moral behavior is defined by and supported by absolutes and is in turn supportive of those absolutes (one perpetuates the other). Related to the idealist concept of the good life is the concept of harmony with super force; therefore, what is moral is that which harmonizes the individual with super force. Leaders, authorities, or wise men have enforcement and interpretive powers in the area of moral behavior. A theocracy is an extreme example of idealist moral principles invested in government and law. Tradition is closely bound to moral teaching and vice versa.

Realism

To the realist the definition of morality is dependent on nature and natural law. Society is to be studied and quantified. Norms based on the sample that has been studied are established. Custom, mores, laws, and morality are derived from societal norms and from what has been demonstrated to be required in order to be in harmony with a society and with nature (of which that social group is a part). Social scientists are the likely sources of data and the interpreters of that data into custom and law.

Pragmatism

When (if) pragmatists speak of morality, they are speaking of something dependent on social interaction and upon the needs and aspirations of individuals and social groups. Unlike idealists, the pragmatists are not speaking of "morality" in the sense of being tied to absolutes which are unchanging or to an everlasting super force. Nor are they speaking of norms derived from studying the operations of humans applying nature's law of interaction (as in economics) for realists. Rather, the pragmatist is more inclined to reintroduce the concepts of practical, utilitarian practices with good outcomes which do not violate democratic principles and processes. The major aim of the pragmatist is the protection of social, civil, and individual rights of all citizens in a changing and relative world. There is a serious attempt to reconcile and harmonize the individual and society for the betterment of each.

Existentialism

To the existentialist the highest moral law is the admonition to become, to Be, to fully develop the authentic self. Any definition of morality is dependent upon the needs and choices of the individual as he or she attempts to achieve that ideal. The goal is internal personal harmony with the self. One is the judge of one's actions and is responsible for the consequences. Social morality may be achieved through the value concept for existentialists "to act (choose) as you would have all men act (choose)."

Decision-Making

Idealism

The idealist basis for making good decisions is set forth in the will of super force (commandments, constitutions, laws, traditions). The design for decision-making and the acceptable limits are prescribed. If one wishes "to be at one with" super force there are steps which must (and must not) be taken. Totally free and independent individual thought is discouraged.

Realism

The realist thinks decisions are best made in accordance with known, tested, observable natural phenomena and the laws which govern those circumstances. Good decisions are those which do not violate laws of the natural physical universe. Individuals are encouraged to think and conduct research, but they are to follow accepted guidelines which are derived from tested procedures, scientific methodology, nature, and physical law.

Pragmatism

Pragmatists believe that decisions have to have practical and useful outcomes to be judged valid. They also may not violate the will or the needs of the majority or violate individual rights under democratic processes. There can be no unquestioned following of the traditions or procedures of the past. One must think for one's self but with a social conscience and concern for outcomes. Scientific methodology and deduction form a major portion of the intellectual foundation of decision-making for pragmatists.

Existentialism

The existentialist places responsibility for being a decision maker and for being responsible for the consequences of choosing upon the shoulders of the individual chooser. While there may be some guidelines, there are no laws or rules to be followed and the individual is ultimately and totally responsible. The individual cannot help but be a decision maker and the ultimate judgment is: "Does this lend authenticity to my being?"

Love

Idealism

Love for the idealist is defined by and comes from super force. The highest love is the love of super force for us and our love of super force (God, the state, nationalism) in return. The traditions, mores, and revered writings portray acceptable models of family love, brotherly love, love between man and woman, and love for country. Maternal love is lauded. Love is an aspect of the human spirit. In super force's model, concern for others may be the epitome of human love.

Realism

For the realist love is physical, genetic, gonadal, or learned behavior and not due to some higher spirituality. Respect (love) for nature is probably the highest love. Nature does not love us in return. Nature provides order and security. Love as the poets describe it is not testable or measurable in any acceptable scientific way, so it is not a proper topic of investigation. Selfless acts to conserve or protect nature may come close to a definition of love.

Pragmatism

The social interaction between individuals is where love is demonstrated and learned for the pragmatist. Living up to the democratic ideal may be considered love for one's fellow human beings (in a broad sense). The pragmatist views the individual as a social, biological, and psychological organism; therefore, love is viewed as influenced by social learning, physical need, and emotional condition. Serving our fellow humans socially or politically becomes a sort of pragmatic model of love.

Existentialism

Love of self and care and concern for personal development are keys to understanding the existentialist concept of love. Existentialists would agree that this is an ego involvement with self, but they would hasten to add that it should not be labeled as "selfish or bad," for they do not mean self at the expense of others. They would contend that knowing, understanding, and loving one's self is necessary before one can reach out to others fully. The existentialist believes that one should act as one would have others act, which may be a form of the Golden Rule. True altruism is difficult for the existentialist to achieve because of the primacy of the ego or self. The existentialist accepts the notions of romantic or brotherly love (and other kinds as well) but always places the thinking, choosing, feeling individual in the center of the design.

The Future

Idealism

The future for idealists is planned and controlled by super force. It may be interpreted by designated authorities. There is a grand plan stretching from our past into the future. Absolutes and universals are everlasting. There may be elements of destiny or ordination in our lives. Some idealists believe in predestination, God's will, or fate and kismet. Human beings can't really do much to influence the future fundamentally; it is viewed essentially as a closed system.

Realism

The future is seen by realists as nature unfolding and evolving according to its laws and plans. Scientific studies and projections provide data for planning. Genetics and evolution are governed by natural law and natural function; therefore, humans must learn nature and understand its laws if they are to have any chance to shape the future. Humans who carry out nature's plan are participating in something outside of their control. Some sort of determinism (essentially biological) is accepted by most realists. For the average person the future is basically a closed system.

Pragmatism

Pragmatists interpret the future as being planned and created as human beings interact in social environments. Humans can adapt themselves to environments as well as change or influence the environment. Change is seen as a constant condition and humans are limited only by their mental abilities and opportunities to learn. The future is perceived as an open system in which humans influence the future and are influenced by events during the passage of time.

Existentialism

For existentialists the future is in the hands of the individual. One's self and one's future are influenced by intelligent or whimsical choices and actions. Humans are potential in motion or accidents looking for a happening and the future is unknown and limitless. The future is an open event.

Culture

Idealism

Idealists view culture as the creation of super force and as the agent of super force. Culture (through education) is the civilizing agent of society. Culture and tradition are inseparable. Culture provides the values, rules, models, and guides for living the good life. Culture, based on the absolutes of super force, is not expected to change.

Realism

Culture to realists is the natural by-product of social interaction. Culture develops as a result of society functioning according to laws of social and behavioral processes. Because of errant variables which might influence it in a particular direction, culture may sometimes be viewed as a corrupting influence. Generally, however, realists view culture as part of nature to be learned and conserved by each new generation, thereby lending stability and security to human society.

Pragmatism

Pragmatists believe that humans create culture through their interactions and the use of their intellect. Human beings and culture have mutually interactive influences. When humans work or live together, they socialize, and culture is the product of their collective thought and experience. If they find better, more efficient ways of doing things, the culture will change to reflect these alterations. Culture has a contemporaneity and changeability.

Existentialism

Existentialists see the individual as responsible for the creation of his or her own culture as choices are made, actions are taken, meaning is attached, and personhood is manifested. It is a matter of personal meaning and relevance. Thus, culture is not determined by external variables and traditions handed down to each generation; it is created as humans exist.

Change

Idealism

Because of the idealist's belief in absolutes, there is a skepticism in regard to change and progress. Change occurs very slowly, if at all, because of the collective weight of what is already known to human experience through the ages. There is a heavy reliance upon tradition, the past human experience, and what is already known. There is a reluctance, bordering on refusal, to accept innovations or technological advancements which contradict the known or the believed.

Realism

Nature has its evolutionary plan. Realists see change (slow, evolutionary change) as inevitable. In science the new hypotheses must be tested and retested to determine their validity and reliability. Only then may changes based upon valid, scientifically-determined facts be instigated. This, too, is a lengthy and time-consuming process. Although there is an avenue for change in realism, it happens slowly and only in accordance with nature's principles.

Pragmatism

The world is characterized by progress and change when it is viewed by pragmatists. Not only is the environment changing, but every time a human being thinks, some of the traditions are in danger. The nature of the human is to engage in simultaneous mutual interaction with the environment. Change as a constant and ongoing process is the key.

Existentialism

Because the existentialists believe that humans continuously define and redefine themselves through their choices and actions, change is an accepted element in personal development and, therefore, in society at large.

Section II

Educational Issues and Topics

In the following pages, the four philosophies of idealism, realism, pragmatism, and existentialism are applied to a broad selection of educational issues and topics. The reader is encouraged to draw comparisons between and among philosophies and to look for philosophic themes covered in Section I.

It is possible, using this volume, to determine a model for schooling as it would operate under each of the four philosophies. It is also likely that the reader will begin to recognize the impact of each of the philosophies on contemporary school programs and practices which may be operational in a given locale at a given time. The American public schools at the present time are a mixture of the various philosophies. The organization, methods, and purposes of the contemporary comprehensive high school, for example, are sometimes a confusing and even contradictory amalgamation of ideas from the four philosophies. Some of these ideas and concepts have been selected almost helter-skelter over more than two hundred years of educational history in response to prevailing social and educational beliefs or occasional fads and bandwagons.

To summarize, this section is intended to help the beginning student of philosophy (as applied to the study of education) find his or her way among the often confusing elements of the American public school. A footnote is appropriate here with respect to private and parochial schools. They too follow no one model but have incorporated practices from a variety of educational and philosophical perspectives.

Purpose(s) of Education

Idealism

To the dedicated idealist the underlying purpose of schooling is to bring uneducated children into harmony with super force so that in their adulthood they will be prepared to contribute to the fulfillment of super force's plan. Important here is to conform harmoniously with the word of super force (the laws, mores, and traditions) and living one's life in the service of super force in an idealist environment. Of course, schools should teach the basic intellectual skills and traditional subjects that idealists know children need in order to become proper adults, but to impart to the young the stories, facts, laws, and traditions about super force carries the highest priority.

Realism

The purpose of education for the realist is to prepare children to live harmoniously with nature when they become adults. Children must be trained to conform to and to understand nature's laws to insure the survival of the species. School should teach respect for nature (life, ecology) and also teach humans to be careful and accurate observers who are dedicated to the use of deductive thinking and the scientific method. Schools should, therefore, teach the scientific method and the known facts and laws of nature and the external world.

Pragmatism

To assist the child toward becoming a socially valuable individual now and in the future is the purpose of education to the pragmatist. If there is conformity, it is to live harmoniously with one's fellows while developing one's individuality. Schools should recognize that children are alive now and that they need help now and in the future with problem-solving skills and understanding their environment and themselves. Pragmatists view the school as society in miniature and, thus, they believe it should teach respect for the democratic, social and political process. Schools should also teach students how to use the scientific process as a means of identifying and solving life's problems. In a larger sense, schools should teach the lifelong skill of knowing how to learn.

Existentialism

The only acceptable purpose for education or school-ing for the existentialist is to help the child become a fully authentic self. The teacher and school should assist the child in the process of becoming an intelli-gent, sensitive, choosing, acting person who recog-nizes the opportunity and the obligation of freedom and exercises it authentically. Important in this proc-ess is helping the individual to identify the self as being separate from the group, family, or team and encourag-ing the emerging selfhood. School should also teach children to identify and evaluate alternatives and to accept responsibility for self-development.

Curriculum Priorities

Idealism

For the idealist the priorities in the curriculum (espe-cially for high school students) are the liberal arts and humanities. Literature, the classics, philosophy, and history as literature are key elements in the idealist curriculum. Here, history as literature means reading history to obtain the story of "our people," understand-ing the adversities that they have overcome and glory-ing in their triumphs. The purpose of the curriculum is to introduce culture, without which man could not become civilized. The curriculum would also include art and music appreciation. The curriculum which is classical or traditional reflects the will of super force. The idealist would be reluctant to introduce students to any subject matter which has not stood the test of time. Subjects (especially literature and history) would be filled with acceptable (to adults) models exemplifying how to live the moral and good life. Subject matter would be carefully chosen to present the highest ideals of the good and proper life to be lived by members of a given idealist community. Stories with a moral, such as Aesop's fables and others where good triumphs over evil and in which "our people" win, would be strong curricular components. The classical trivium (grammar, rhetoric, and logic) is the ancestor of the modern idealist curriculum.

(All four philosophies believe in the necessity of learning the "tool subjects" of reading, writing, and computation, although the reader will discover that they would teach them differently.)

Realism

The realist is most interested in a curriculum which is founded on and contributes to the study of nature. Biological and physical sciences, mathematics, and the social sciences would form the cornerstones of the curriculum. Mathematics in the realist curriculum would consist of algebra, geometry, trigonometry, and calculus. To the realist, the social sciences represent the discrete and isolated study of human behavior by applying science to the study of different aspects of human behavior. This encompasses such courses as sociology, anthropology, political science, economics, geography, and the objective study of history. In this sense there are specialists in social sciences just as there are in the physical and biological sciences. The classical quadrivium is the ancestor of the modern realist curriculum. The quadrivium was composed of arithmetic, geometry, astronomy, and music. The subjects in the curriculum would be the real stuff of nature.

Pragmatism

The pragmatist is not much concerned with the presentation of a curriculum which is selected by adults and which may be traditional and time tested. The pragmatist sees curriculum not as a list of subjects, but rather as skills and processes to be learned. The pragmatist curriculum would be composed of such elements as social studies (not social sciences), the manual and practical arts, problem solving, living skills, language arts (not discrete English classes), American or human problems, citizenship (not political science), and consumer skills classes. The criteria for approving curricula might be stated in such questions as: Does it teach problem solving, is it practical, is it utilitarian, does it have relevance in terms of how a child of a given age views the world, will it help students make sense of their world now and in the future and help them figure out how to improve their lot and society's?

Existentialism

The whole issue of curriculum to the existentialist is a difficult one to grasp because, in a very real sense, the existentialist would permit almost any subject in which the student was truly interested. However, there are types of classes which the existentialist believes do a better job of focusing on the human predicament than others. The key courses in the curriculum would probably be courses such as the fine arts, drama, creative expression, literature, and philosophy. The focus would be on the absurdities of existence, the authentic life, examining and developing self and personhood, rather than studying them as the idealist might—learning facts, memorizing passages, and imitating the style of the masters.

Curricular Emphasis

Idealism

The idealist emphasizes those curricular elements which are cognitive and based upon knowledge and fact. The idealist curriculum is based on the firm foundation of traditionally accepted practice. There is also emphasis on the skills necessary to utilize and manipulate words and facts.

Realism

The realist also emphasizes the curricular elements which are cognitive and based upon knowledge and fact but does so from a different perspective. The realist is prone to reach the facts and knowledge through both words (lectures, essays, readings) and things (audiovisual materials, demonstrations, etc.). There is a concern for development of skills in the utilization of knowledge.

Pragmatism

The pragmatist emphasizes the content and the processes of thinking and problem solving by relying upon a problem-solving curricular format in which knowledge of how to analyze problems and seek solutions is as important as knowledge of facts and content. The pragmatist focuses upon process and upon development of attitudes (particularly democratic ones) and skills in learning and problem solving.

Existentialism

The existentialist emphasizes the affective curricular elements. Content is not viewed as unimportant, but the individual's development of relevance and meaning is more important than learning unemotional or nonpersonal facts. The development of the individual's knowledge, emotions, and attitudes about self, others, and super force are important elements in the existential curriculum.

Approach to Subject Matter

Idealism

The idealist approach to subject matter is quite structured. The classical religious concept of learning one's catechism would be a fair historical model. Curriculum is traditional and viewed as unchanging and rigid. The idealist curriculum is based upon pre-existent reality (from super force).

Realism

The realist envisions subject matter as fixed by the limits of human understanding of nature. The realist is quite likely to have structured curriculum guides and course outlines and the teacher is expected to adhere rigidly to them. The realist curriculum is based upon the external reality of nature.

Pragmatism

The pragmatist approach to subject matter is influenced by a commitment to a process orientation. Pragmatic subject matter is amorphous and hard to pin down because of the accent on flexibility and cur-

ricular innovation to meet the social needs of society
and the felt needs of individual students.

Existentialism

The existentialist also sees the subject matter amor-
phously because it is seen as important only when it is
personally meaningful. It is an individualized curriculum designed for the individual's search for personhood. The existential curriculum is based upon personal need.

Subject Matter and Knowledge

Idealism

Knowledge is viewed by the idealist as being finite
and known perfectly only to super force. Knowledge is
revealed to us through histories, holy works, venerated
political documents and by the authorities who interpret them. The closer one is to super force, the closer one
is to perfect knowledge. Adults are closer than children
to super force (because of education and longevity);
therefore, they learn the knowledge and hand it down
generation to generation.

Realism

Realists deal with the objectivity of knowledge which
can be acquired by observing and understanding
nature through scientific methodology. The realist
believes that the student who applies science carefully,
and well, will be able to know nature without error.
Like the idealist, the realist believes that adults have

more knowledge and that their responsibility is to teach it to the young, who are naive and uneducated.

Pragmatism

To the pragmatists knowledge is constantly being created, remodeled, used, and abandoned. Knowledge per se is less important than thinking (or at least no more important). Thinking is the realignment of ideas and experience (knowledge). Teachers are more knowledgeable than students but do not dictate. Pragmatist teachers and students create, use, and exchange knowledge together.

Existentialism

Existentialists are convinced of the subjectivity of knowledge. They see knowledge through personal relevance with the self as the ultimate reference. Existentialists believe that one can learn with and from a variety of sources and do not conform to a standard approach to knowledge or to curriculum. The most important subject matter is that which leads one to being (and to authentic selfhood).

Role of the Teacher

Idealism

In defining the proper role of the teacher, idealists would stress the importance of exhibiting the highest levels of moral goodness and scholarship. The teacher is to be the interpreter of super force's laws and will, as well as the ultimate authority. Other roles which fit the idealist teacher are the role of mentor (wise advisor) or revealer of the unknown. The teacher is expected to be a somewhat charismatic persuader and inspiring academic leader well versed in the use of words.

Realism

Realists expect teachers to be a good model of a well-trained adult, able to use scientific methods and exemplify scholarship. The realist teacher is considered an authority with superior knowledge as well as the master and explainer of the unknown. As the conduit through which the knowledge of nature reaches the student, the realist teacher tries to organize instruction and present the curriculum free of his or her own personality.

Pragmatism

The pragmatist teacher is a fellow participant, experienced student, guide, and facilitator of the learning process. The examples pragmatists expect teachers to portray are those of respecters of individual rights and practitioners of democratic processes. They are also to be model problem-solvers and appropriate users of scientific methods. The teacher's role is to motivate, influence, and facilitate learning.

Existentialism

The existentialist would probably most expect the teacher to portray authentic adulthood in the form of a fellow traveler on the continuous quest for selfhood. The teacher is a questioner, poser of alternatives, and identifier of choices who challenges the student to

Become. The existentialist teacher is seen as one half of a dialogue.

Methods of Instruction

Idealism

The methods of instruction preferred by the idealist are basically those which are dependent upon words—heard, spoken, written, or read. Lecture heads the list of techniques, closely followed by recitation, essay writing, rote memorization, and assigned readings. The idealist works primarily with whole group instruction and relies on individual pupil effort.

Realism

The realist also relies upon words but supports them with things to be handled, manipulated, viewed, or tested. Lecture, recitation, and essays are central elements combined with instructional media, laboratory work, demonstrations, field trips, and research papers. The realist was the first to support the written words in textbooks with pictures and diagrams. Like the idealist, the realist teacher relies on large group instruction and depends on individual pupil effort and motivation.

Pragmatism

The pragmatist teacher relies on teacher-facilitated student activity as a mainstay of instruction. Problem solving, role playing, and dramatization, active participation, discussion, and group work are some of the ways the pragmatist puts the concept of "learning by doing" into practice. The teacher uses a variety of methods to get students to invest themselves and their energies in learning in order to realize the greatest possible returns. In instruction the pragmatist uses various sizes of groups, based on student interest and need, to capitalize on the social side of human nature, thus encouraging student involvement.

Existentialism

The existentialist teacher encourages individual expression, promotes individual activity, and utilizes voluntary grouping patterns. There is a dependence on dialogue, the Socratic method, dramatic presentations, creative activity, and individual readings. The teacher tries to promote an "encounter" between and among students, knowledge, and the search for self in order to establish individual meaning and relevance.

Schools and Teachers as Agents of Change

Idealism

The idealist often proclaims that school is not the appropriate vehicle for promoting social or cultural change. Schools are expected to preserve the best from the past, promote the status quo, and contribute to social stability. Since the idealist reveres tradition, school is meant to teach the traditions of the group and the time-tested and accepted absolutes and rituals. When the idealist functions as a missionary, he or she does not see this as promoting spiritual, cultural, or social change; rather it is seen as extending the status quo to encompass new beings who need it. School does change children, but in "acceptable" ways.

Realism

The realist is reluctant to see change that is unwarranted or unsupported by data or research. There should be no change merely for the sake of change because nature is more orderly than that. Nature uses evolution as its basic change process. Rapid change should still be tested and verified through objective scientific processes. Children should learn respect for the order that is found in nature and respect for the scientific method. Children will be changed by school from ignorant to knowledgeable beings.

Pragmatism

The pragmatist accepts being a change agent as a reasonable role in a world of change. The teacher will describe the status quo, but will not advocate it unconditionally because it won't last forever, and it may or may not be useful to students as they try to identify and solve their problems in the present or in the future. If teachers teach learning strategies and ways of thinking rather than teaching what to think, students can participate deliberately in creating, sustaining, or changing their worlds. The pragmatist tries to teach alternative ways of thinking, searching, and problem solving rather than rules, facts, rituals, catechisms, and laws. Pragmatists are committed to "process" and ongoing activities, rather than static conditions.

Existentialism

Because individuals are changing and growing rapidly as they act and choose in the process of defining themselves, the existentialist is in the position of establishing an environment or climate which allows change but which does not deliberately provoke it. Existentialists cannot be true existentialists and also be evangelists or missionaries actively promoting recruitment to existentialism. They can, however, initiate and nurture a climate of openness within which students feel free to make a variety of personally meaningful choices.

Permanence and Change

Idealism

The idealist believes that there is permanence in super force. The idealist accepts the idea that there are absolutes which amount to believing in truth and seeing virtually no room for change. If super force is perfect and all-knowing, then there can be little opportunity for new knowledge. The idealist is preparing students to live in a world in which virtually all that is knowable and worth knowing is already known by the elder generation which has written it down or is willing to tell it. If students study diligently, read appropriately, and listen to their elders, they will learn everything they need to know.

Realism

The realist finds permanence in nature, in its laws,

principles, and orderliness. The realist believes that there are eternal truths in nature that will never change. The only opportunities for new knowledge come through technological breakthroughs in our observation techniques and measurement tools or through learning about previously unknown interactions among nature's parts through experimentation or introducing new variables. Thus, there is little room for change in the basics—and that only after extensive testing. Furthermore, curriculum and teaching techniques will change very little, except for fine tuning or refinement, without extensive testing of the "innovations."

Pragmatism

Flux and change and the absence of absolutes are the concepts that influence pragmatists. Pragmatists have enough respect for scientific method that they will not encourage serendipitous change or change for its own sake. Changes must be warranted and serve practical purposes. The pragmatist is a relativist taking into account the environment as well as the individual's perceptions of it when making decisions. The teacher is bound to few (if any) of the guidelines ruling the realist or idealist teacher. Children are introduced to alternatives and to a variety of perspectives. The pragmatist school is more open to change, allowance for change, and encouraging students to seek controversial areas than its more traditional counterparts.

Existentialism

The existentialist world is centered on personal

meaning and relevance. Personalization is the key, with flexibility based on individual emotion and reason. This opens the educational enterprise to change both for the student and the teacher. The limiting factors for both are that (1) they must accept all of the consequences of their behavior, and (2) they are responsible for being in charge of their lives and for making free and authentic choices.

Teacher's Power Roles

Idealism

The teacher's power in idealism comes from the traditionally defined role of the teacher and from the authority delegated by the school board, superintendent, and principal to the teacher. There is also the traditional relationship of adults who have knowledge and children who do not. The teacher is also the exemplar of the ideal (super force). The concept of en loco parentis is an idealist concept with teachers standing in the place of the parent and having similar powers and responsibilities.

Realism

The teacher in realism has traditionally been the key figure and the authoritarian in the classroom. Naturally adults are superior to children because of education, experience, and longevity. Again, as with idealism, realists believe that adults know and children do not know. The teacher is the exemplar of reality (nature).

Pragmatism

Pragmatists interpret teacher power differently in that they see it not as coercive or authoritative power (as do idealists and realists) but rather as persuasive and practical. The pragmatist is committed to the use of democratic and non-authoritarian power methods (a la Thomas Gordon). Adults share responsibility and power with children while teaching them how to use it effectively. In a power parity relationship the teacher is a guide rather than an authority. The teacher uses the natural authority of experience, skill, and expertise.

Existentialism

In a non-authoritarian environment the existentialist teacher shares responsibility with students as co-equals. This shared sense of individual responsibility encourages individual choice and participation in dialogue. Teachers are powerful only as students see them as meaningful or relevant to their lives and goals. Teachers use the power of their personality and knowledge of (and their involvement with) subject matter to influence the student's behavior in non-directive ways.

School Rules

Idealism

The rules of school in idealism are based in tradition and in what is known to be good for children. They are time-tested rules and policies, and they are made by the adults in charge. There are very few exceptions to idealist rules and there is little room for changing them. They appear rigid and inflexible and usually include penalties for infractions. The teachers enforce them.

Realism

When realists make the rules for school, their rules are likely to be based on the norms of previous classes and upon what the "authorities or experts" say is sound practice (based upon the norms from their research). Few exceptions to the rules are allowed, and when they are, carefully detailed procedures have to be followed. Those procedures are often extremely rigorous and cumbersome, resulting in little actual change. Penalties for infraction are often included in the policies; teachers are the enforcers.

Pragmatism

The pragmatist works out the classroom and school rules through joint democratic action in class meetings with both teacher and students stating their needs and their expectations. There is room for exceptions through a process of referendum or negotiation if the rule does not prove to be workable. Penalties are negotiable depending on a variety of variables. Enforcement of rules and policies is the job of both teachers and students. In some cases there are even student courts or appeals groups. The purpose is not only to teach the rules, but the pragmatist wants to teach about rule making and understanding personal and social implications of both violating the rules and being law-abiding.

Existentialism

The existentialist is less in favor of school rules and more inclined to favor individual responsibility. Teachers may engage students in discussion (dialogue) on topics such as "What do we as individuals need to do in order to get along, accomplish our goals, safeguard our freedom?" The existentialist teacher also makes sure that the student understands the possible and probable (as well as preferable) consequences of behavior and also tries to insure that the student expresses in advance the understanding of his or her own responsibilities.

Expectations for Learners

Idealism

The idealist expects students to be obedient and scholarly, cooperative and respectful (reverent). Children are expected to be little adults with knowledge of good and bad already available to them (innate), but because they are immature, they let badness (evil, devil) take charge because they have not learned self-discipline. The idealist adults expect some misbehavior and are prepared for it with the rules and punishments that have been used to discipline students in the past.

Realism

Realists view students not as little adults but more as

little animals to be tamed, domesticated, trained, or socialized. The realist teacher expects students to obey and be scholarly, to conform to rules and social norms, and to carry out assignments in an organized and orderly manner. The realist relies on training schedules, sequencing subject matter, reinforcement schedules, and routines to accomplish the tasks of domestication.

Pragmatism

The pragmatist teacher expects students to exhibit curiosity, be active participants in school processes, and be socially responsible for their actions. They are expected to learn, experience, try out new ideas, and examine behaviors. Since this describes a more flexible view of the nature of the child than does either idealism or realism, it is also expected that there are fewer parameters or limits for student behavior.

Existentialism

The existentialist teacher expects the student to be a questioner of life and its events. Students are choice-makers who are creating themselves. They are also expected to be independent, free-thinking beings who are responsible for the consequences of their choices. The existentialist feels that labeling behavior as being "good" or "bad" is not productive since those are society's labels which are meaningless to individuals. What is more important is "What are the consequences?" "Who is responsible?" "How can I influence my own behavior in the future?"

Preferred Student Role

Idealism

The prevalent idealist preference for student behavior is defined by the weight of idealist history and tradition. The student's role is essentially a passive one in which the student carries out orders. The student most prized is the one who accurately predicts the teacher's wishes and correctly and efficiently fulfills them at a level of superior competence (for a student).

Realism

Realist teachers prefer students who respond appropriately when stimulated by methodology and curriculum. This describes a reactive role in which the student is the obedient receiver and responder. The prized student is the one whose interests parallel those of the teacher and whose questions are the ones the teacher wants asked and whose observations and generalizations are usable to the teacher in teaching other students.

Pragmatism

Pragmatist teachers prefer those students with sufficient social skill, communication ability, and strength of ego to engage successfully in give and take and classroom debates and discussions while solving problems independently or with others. The student is encouraged to be curious and interactive. The student is a receiver, responder, and an initiator. Prized students are the ones who create innovative, sound, practical solutions to problems, who eagerly seek new challenges and opportunities to gain new experience, and test themselves individually and socially while respecting the rights of others.

Existentialism

The existentialist teacher is looking for students who are self-initiators, who are actually involved in determining their lives, and who are both sensitive and curious when it comes to understanding self and one's fellow human beings. Students are to reach out intellectually, physically, and emotionally for selfhood (and to others as an expression of self). Prized students are those who eagerly initiate personally meaningful learning in the search for authentic selfhood—asking and answering probing questions about the human condition, creating and expressing their selfhood in self-relevant ways, and engaging widely in dialogue in a search for experiences from which to construct their authentic being.

Individual Differences

Idealism

Idealists tend to see all beings as equal in the sight of super force; therefore, there is little real concern for individual differences. There is little individualization. Everyone is expected to listen to the same lecture, read the same material, and work on the same assignment at the same time. If they don't, then standards become meaningless. The student is expected to conform to the rules and to live up to the teacher's high behavioral and academic standards. Those students who cannot meet the standards (for whatever reasons) are left gradually behind their classmates, and any remediation will occur when they take the same course again next year and go through the material for a second time.

Realism

The realist studied human beings as no one ever did before. Years were spent gathering data in a variety of research designs to determine the averages and ranges of a whole host of human measurements. There is some tracking (grouping but no individualizing) based on test data. The tracking tends to be into broad groups (high, middle, and low). Special education for extremely low ability students may well have had its origins in realism. The student is expected to conform to the social norms of his or her group. Like idealism, realism may well lead to the formation of a corps of intellectually or academically elite students with less able classmates being left behind in lower groups with less opportunity and challenge.

Pragmatism

The pragmatist seeks out and attempts to capitalize on individual interests, needs, and abilities since these factors influence the curriculum and the methodology. Motivation and activity must be individually tailored as students choose projects, roles, and problems to solve. There is activity in a variety of types and sizes of groups to help individuals learn social and communication skills which are vital to success in a democratic environment. The group is an avenue through which the individual can develop.

Existentialism

For the existentialist teacher the individual exists before all else. The choices that the individual makes determine content and methods. There is heavy emphasis on individual activities; individual responsibility for choice is emphasized also. Individual research and creativity are advocated, and so too is the dialogue as a method of enhancing selfhood through a one-to-one encounter between selves.

Individual Student Rights

Idealism

Idealist tradition, sacred or revered documents, and historical precedent define social and political roles of all groups including children and youth. The state or God (super force) comes first along with authorized interpreters and spokesmen. Adults, especially educated and authorized adults, have total power over subordinates (including children). There is a power system established in which adults and other social groups have power and children do not have power. Historically in idealism, women and children have been chattel or property and, thus, have had very few rights. Children are not to be entrusted with making significant educational or life decisions.

Realism

The realist perspective on student rights and individualism is largely based on a biological or sociological view of human beings in which the individual is viewed as a part of a greater system with no part automatically being greater or more important than another. Status is achieved with longevity and intellectual achievement; thus, adults have the advantage over children and youth by virtue of their age and experience. Children are to do as the experienced members tell them to do. The realist is often more interested in group data than with individual lives. Adults make decisions for their less mature and less capable charges.

Pragmatism

The individual in a democratic setting has rights but cannot exercise them at others' expense. The concept of equality before the law, which emerged from realist philosophy in the sixteenth century, is extended by pragmatists to children and youth on a reasonable scale. Children have rights in schools and classrooms; there is a greater power parity between children and adults in pragmatism than with either idealism or realism. Since the child is to learn about democracy (rights, freedoms, responsibilities, and duties) by practicing it in schools, the practice of it must be legitimate and students must really have some freedom of choice and action. Adults still have a role and a voice, but it is no longer the voice of the dictator (no matter how benevolent). They are, rather, guides or more experienced colleagues giving useful information and reminders.

Existentialism

The individual's freedom is primary to everything in existentialism. The existentialist extends to students the freedom to be and to become all that their potential will allow. Children share in the concept of total freedom. Individual thought and responsibility are encouraged. This is not to say that existentialists would place naive, inexperienced "choosers" in a health or life threatening choice situation and make them suffer the consequences of their decisions. There is, however, a willingness to let students experience more of life's variety of choices (at sophistication levels they can handle).

Discipline Expectations

Idealism

The idealist teacher is the authority and in charge of the classroom. Student obedience and respect are required. Some misbehavior is expected from students who have not learned self-discipline. Teachers have rules and punishments to handle students who need more discipline training. Discipline is achieved by doing difficult tasks to train the mind and which discipline the body to the will of the mind. Adults know what is best and teachers set the rules and tell them to students who either obey the rules or suffer the punishments. Discipline is largely external and it is intended to encourage recognition of the ideals of super force. Eventually the student is expected to internalize the discipline. The younger or more unsophisticated the learner, the more extrinsic means are needed.

Realism

The realist teacher relies upon behaviorism, reinforcement, extinction, behavior modification, successive approximations and habit formation to operate a discipline program. Teachers set the rules and students obey them with reinforcements appropriate to the task and behavior being applied on a schedule. Adults know best and they try to apply discipline which is objective, unemotional, fair, and consistent. Discipline which is largely external and controlled by adults does not require individual understanding of its basis. It is believed that through reinforcement and repetition the extrinsic discipline will ultimately be internalized and the result will be self-discipline.

Pragmatism

The pragmatist teacher and students mutually define the rules and also the punishments or consequences for violating them. There is a reliance upon student councils to give students a positive voice in governance and sometimes student courts or student participation on panels or committees listening to student appeals. One limitation to all of this is that democratic procedures be followed, that no one's rights be violated, and that each person have a proportionate share of power (one person-one vote). There is a concern that there be "natural" and reasonable consequences for misbehavior. Discipline is interactive and requires individual participation and insight. Students are expected to be involved in disciplining themselves as a means of contributing to a positive social climate for all (internal and external).

Existentialism

Existentialist discipline is individually determined and based on individual acceptance of consequences of actions. Discipline is essentially "internal" and within the control of the student. Disciplinary policy (if one existed) would probably be one of permissiveness, and students would be expected to accept the results of both good and bad choices.

Discipline Models

Idealism

"Spare the rod and spoil the child" is the most often-quoted discipline model of idealist parents and teachers. The idealist model relies on rules, rewards, and punishments. It is a model with the weight of history and tradition behind it. Part of it is based on the belief that self-discipline is learned by doing hard tasks that one does not wish to do (or from learning difficult subjects). The idealist will permit corporal punishment ("This hurts me more than it hurts you" and "Some day you will understand why I'm having to do this and you will thank me"). There is a belief that rehabilitation is dependent to a major degree upon punishment. The most popular contemporary spokesperson of the idealist position on discipline is James Dobson.

Realism

The realist relies upon behaviorism and behavior modification strategies including reinforcement schedules and extinction of behavior to discipline students. Many of the elements in Canter's *Assertive Discipline* fit the realist model of teacher proposed rules, reinforcements for obeying these rules, and corrective sequences to be followed for persistent misbehaviors. The basic work of B.F. Skinner is drawn upon heavily by the realist teacher who is looking to behavior analysis for the key to unlocking student behavior and learning.

Pragmatism

Because pragmatists see the school and the classroom as a miniature society, it is reasonable to expect them to apply as much democratic procedure in their discipline model as possible. They give the student a voice and a vote. The practical element comes in through the concept of natural consequences advocated by Driekurs. Dewey's work and influence can also be seen in the ideas of student involvement in, and ownership of, the rules they establish through democratic process and the development of the possible negative consequences of violating the rules.

Existentialism

The openness of Summerhill School as described by A. S. Neill would probably suffice as a model for existential education and discipline. The Summerhill model with its permissiveness and apparent lack of structure relies upon the student to choose wisely and in time (eventually) encounter and learn what is vital and meaningful to the individual. Some of the elements of open spaces, open classrooms, free schools, and alternative schools are efforts to put students more in the center of their lives, their education, and their development of themselves as responsible choosing beings.

Students with Special Needs

Idealism

The idealist's primary focus is on academically talented students. There are academic standards that need to be met, and the task of a school is to meet or exceed those standards. The student with learning problems or social or personal difficulties is expected to try to meet these standards. There are few provisions other than "trade schools" for the non-academically talented student. The student who fails and falls behind is "just not academic material." There is a fairly high dropout rate among the students with special learning needs. Academically talented students are pushed as far and as fast as possible, either skipping grades or getting an enriched educational opportunity.

Realism

The greatest concern of realists is also for academically talented students (especially in science and math). Although realists have gathered lots of data on human development, stages of development, normalcy, and abnormalcy, and although they talk much about individual differences, they do not do much with what they know. There is some tracking in the basic subjects (into high, middle, and low or remedial classes.) There is also some use of special education classes.

Pragmatism

Pragmatists believe that vocational-technical programs, life-oriented courses, and college preparatory

and advanced placement programs take care of the
needs of some "special" students. Other individual differences for other students are met through social or
life adjustment curricula. There is a variety of special-
needs classes and mainstreaming for those who can
profit from it. The rights of all students are protected
including their right to education appropriate to their
condition in the least restrictive environment.

Existentialism

The design preferred by existentialism would be
complete individualization and one-to-one instruction.
This would take care of any student needs that a
teacher might encounter. Admittedly this is expensive
if not impossible, say the existentialists, but this is the
goal. The existentialist emphasizes the rights of all
students to a quality education appropriate to their
needs and talents. This is an area that existentialism
addresses only in the broadest terms.

Type of Thinking Prized

Idealism

To the idealist the learning of facts and verbal
abstractions is of primary importance. Rote memorization is also important because of what it contributes to
learning important facts. Traditional subject matter is
to be learned efficiently and economically. The student
learns convergent thinking and Aristotelian logic.
Inductive thought processes are respected.

Realism

The realist is more concerned about memorization of scientific facts or structural principles and their subsequent application. Divergent thinking is important and related to scientific methodology. The deductive thought processes are advocated. The goal is for a student to possess a quantity of facts and be capable of using them scientifically.

Pragmatism

Students in pragmatist schools are encouraged to engage in intelligent problem solving and searching for alternative solutions. Divergent thinking and scientific methods are used in problem solving. The thinking design is experimental, utilizing the approach of science combined with a practical approach aimed at getting the job done. It tends toward flexibility and non-traditional outcomes.

Existentialism

For the existentialists the individual exists, chooses, and thinks. They advocate divergent thinking and creative, intuitive responses. The type of thinking respected is best described as abstract-personal.

Who Has Knowledge

Idealism

The idealist believes that knowledge is in books (curriculum) and is best obtained through formal education. Ultimately knowledge comes from super force. Adults have knowledge because they have education, and children don't because they are unsophisticated and uneducated. Adults pass this knowledge on to succeeding generations which amounts to a cultural rebirth in each new generation.

Realism

Realists believe also that knowledge is in the curriculum and found in books and in objective observation. Knowledge comes from nature. Adults have knowledge and their task is to pass that knowledge on to each new generation of naive students. Formal education is viewed as the best vehicle for acquiring knowledge. Both idealism and realism are somewhat skeptical of education which is not based on traditional academic concepts and methods. So-called "life experience" curricula or the "school of hard knocks" are poor substitutes for the academic classrooms.

Pragmatism

Pragmatist teachers see children as active participants in the learning process using their own experiences, classmates' experiences, the library, the laboratory, and the teacher's knowledge as learning resources. With this wealth of information and experience the student can create, recreate, reconstruct, or reconstitute knowledge and give it increased social impact. Knowledge is not a thing or a goal; it is a process, and both students and teachers are involved in it.

Existentialism

Like the pragmatist, the existential teacher sees the

student as a co-equal. The teacher is an example of an independent learner. Children and youth can know and have knowledge as they attach meaning or relevance to the events and experiences of their world and their classroom. Teachers cannot give knowledge to students. Through their actions and choices students make knowledge personal and, thus, grasp it for themselves.

Who Is In Charge

Idealism

In the idealist classroom there is high teacher control. The teacher selects content, method, sequence, rules, discipline, rewards, and punishments—everything. Students make few decisions and contribute little to the organization or function of the classroom. The teacher is in charge.

Realism

Realist teachers are in charge of the classroom or laboratory. Their degree of control is high. The teacher is the organizer and sequencer of all learning activities. The teacher is the master planner of all student behavior. If the teachers do their jobs well, they can predict and control student behavior in advance. Students may be more active than in an idealist class, but they have no more control of the learning space or activities.

Pragmatism

In the pragmatist teacher's classroom there is a

partnership that exists between teacher and students.
Together they select the problems to solve and topics to
study. The sharing of control or the establishment of
parity gives students rights in a democratic setting.
There can be no anarchy. The teacher cannot delegate
all responsibility to the students, but does act as a
guide or facilitator rather than as a director or
ringmaster.

Existentialism

In existentialist classrooms, teaching-learning
encounters are the central feature. Students have more
control than in any of the other three classrooms.
There is relatively high student control of curriculum,
method, and sequence and relatively low teacher control. The teacher's control function is limited to raising
questions, alternatives, and assisting with resource
management.

Classroom Center

Idealism

The idealist classroom is centered on the curriculum
of the humanities. Because curriculum, books, and
knowledge cannot speak for themselves, the teacher as
the interpreter and spokesperson for the curriculum
often seems to occupy the center of the idealist classroom. The idealist classroom is teacher-curriculum
centered.

Realism

The realist classroom is focused on the subject matter of the natural world. The teacher presents and speaks for the curriculum to the student. Although the realist teacher may seem to be the center, the curriculum and the teacher are co-centers with the student involved carrying out teacher-planned activities.

Pragmatism

The pragmatist classroom is process-centered. It may also be described as activity-centered, and since students help plan, execute, and evaluate the activities and processes, it may also be considered student centered. Because teachers do not abdicate responsibility for planning and teaching but share it, the best conceptualization of the center of the pragmatist classroom would probably be teacher-student centered or relational.

Existentialism

The existential classroom is person-centered with the emerging self of the student as the central focus of all classroom and teacher activity. The student as thinker, feeler, chooser, and being is the determiner of what gets learned. The teacher as a person plays a supportive role.

Accountability

Idealism

Idealists hold themselves accountable to excellence and high academic standards. They are responsible to the history and revered traditions of their people. As an agent of super force they follow the traditional liberal arts model. The idealist teacher's goal is to provide the ideal education so children can grow into ideal adults, making an ideal society (the fulfillment of super force's plan) possible. They try to live up to that demanding mental and spiritual challenge.

Realism

Realist teachers are responsible as agents of nature to the society they represent and to academic excellence. Personal scholarship and objectivity are hard taskmasters. They utilize standardized test scores and norms to determine the success of their organizing and programming. They make comparisons with the society, with past performance, and with other groups to measure their own competence.

Pragmatism

The pragmatist teacher is accountable to the society and to the individuals comprising that social group. They use some testing but more for individual diagnosis for remediation or planning than for group evaluation. The ultimate responsibility is to the question: Are we improving individuals who, in turn, can contribute to the improvement of society? The pragmatist is also accountable to operate democratically and to judge worth in terms of practicability and utility.

Existentialism

For the existentialist teacher the emerging individual self of the school child is the only valid external standard for accountability, and this is subjectively determined. Another level of accountability is internal.

It is the teacher's knowledge and sense of his or her own being and authenticity in the teaching encounter and dialogue. The teacher must always be true to self.

Teaching: Art or Science?

Idealism

The idealist teacher may work to develop his or her craft but tends to think of teaching, and especially lecturing, as an art form which evokes student insights and learning. Teaching consists of a mixture of personality, intellect, and art in a uniquely creative effort.

Realism

The realist sees teaching as the application of science methodology through the eyes of Herbart. Teaching is broken down and analyzed task by task, technique by technique, measured and evaluated and reassembled as a mechanic or technician would reassemble a television set or automobile to make it effective and productive.

Pragmatism

For pragmatist teachers the question of art or science is probably not a legitimate question because they do not see teaching in isolation from learning. They see learning and experiencing as more important than teaching. Advocates of this philosophy see teaching and learning as an interactive process incorporating technical skill, artistry, and intuition. The ultimate test is not "Was it appreciated?" "Was it artistic?" or

"Was it pretty?" but rather, "Did it work?" "Did it accomplish our goals?" and "Did it contribute?"

Existentialism

The existentialist sees teaching as an art form (probably as a duet) featuring dialogue, challenge, and a personal (and possibly emotive) encounter between teacher and student as selves who together are exploring questions, creating answers, and attaching meaning.

Objectives

Idealism

In an idealist school general goals and objectives and specific course objectives are established by adults and approved by the administration (and usually the school board). The criteria for judging the suitability of goals are derived from their degree of conformance to classical or traditional models of education. Adults know what students need to learn; therefore, adults set the objectives, the standards of performance, and the rules. Idealists rely on curriculum guides and text materials for course organization. Broad goals and global teacher objectives are the typical style used by idealist educators.

Realism

In realist schools the goals and objectives (long-range and specific) are set by the adults who are knowledgeable in the subject matter and well informed about human development. The planning of goals is objective and scientific. Goals will probably be written in behavioral terms. As in idealism, there is the expectation in realism that adults know what students need to learn.

Pragmatism

In pragmatism there are some goals which are set by adults, but the intermediate and short-range objectives are jointly developed by teachers and students with provisions for negotiation of ends and means as may prove necessary or as situations vary from student to student. Adults and children plan together for what will be learned and how the learning will be accomplished and demonstrated. Objectives are usually stated in individual student outcomes with a time line for completion and checkpoints along the way.

Existentialism

Planning in existentialism is even more flexible than in the pragmatist classroom. Learning goals are selected by students depending on their own needs and understandings. Adults can participate in helping students decide individually what they want to learn or learn about. The adult role is to engage in dialogue with young people, to ask questions, or to motivate. The student must set his or her own objectives because when objectives are written by others and imposed on the individual they may lead to conformity and inauthenticity.

Back to the Basics

Idealism

When the idealists talk about going back to the basics, they are not referring just to the tool subjects or the 3 R's; they are also referring to the humanities and the liberal arts. Invariably they also imply a return to higher academic standards and a return to "excellence."

Realism

For the realist the concept of back to the basics includes emphasis on the tool subjects for basic academic participation and also a renewed emphasis on math and science and sometimes social science. Realists, too, imply the need to return to earlier and higher academic standards.

Pragmatism

A return to basics for pragmatists includes not only the tool subjects (3 R's) but also practical, consumer, citizenship, and survival courses (some elements of which might also be in the social studies curriculum). The emphasis is on meeting students' needs and teaching problem solving.

Existentialism

The existentialist's return to basics would include the tool subjects and anything that would sharpen the student's focus of selfhood, especially the creative and performing arts, the humanities, and personally selected life-relevant courses.

Examinations and Testing

Idealism

The favorite testing procedures among idealists would include recitation or catechism-type oral execises and the writing of essays. The idealist teacher often gives instructions for the latter which include encouraging the student to be creative or original; however, the student is expected to use standard essay format, present prescribed or accepted information in acceptable ways, conform to the prevailing social philosophy, and live up to the teacher's performance expectation. The teacher is the judge of the quality of student performance, and quality is evaluated against an external standard of excellence. The teacher's efforts may be highly subjective. The idealist believes in formal testing as a means of comparing student performance with a standard of excellence. Tests serve vital functions to separate the academically talented from the less talented others.

Realism

Realists rely on objective and standardized tests for the bulk of their examinations of student performance. The modern realist would make the tests criterion-referenced, which would enhance their validity and reliability. They would also submit the tests themselves to item analysis and other statistical evaluation. The realist teacher would compare student scores with norms to determine the degree of excellence achieved. Laboratory tests would also be used as would occasional essays. The realist, like the idealist, would rely on externally determined standards of performance based on cutoff scores and other statistical indicators. The testing would be quite formal, structured, and very serious business. Realists introduced the whole "testing movement" and refined achievement tests to determine grade placement and other indexes of performance.

Pragmatism

When it comes to testing, pragmatists are not as concerned with the student's ability to remember facts, formulae, or functions (idealism and realism) as they are with the question of whether or not the student can solve real problems. Therefore they rely upon problem-solving, project methods, student performance, and other activity-centered methods through which the teacher can determine by firsthand observation whether or not the student can apply the principles and explain the concepts at work. Both individual and group work are examined in this way. Does the student's proposed solution solve the problem? The testing is an informal, on-the-spot, hands-on, practical application of what has been experienced in new settings. Written work (essays) would be sparsely used and would describe solutions to problems. Testing for the pragmatist teacher would be less for determining meritorious scholarship and more for diagnosing how well the teacher taught and how well the student learned to apply the teaching.

Existentialism

For the existentialist, teacher evaluation of students is conducted for the individual student's benefit (if at all). Through dialogue, student-produced work, and self-evaluated work the student answers the following kinds of questions: Is this satisfying? Does it meet some need? Does it lead me to an authentic expression of myself? Did I accomplish what I wanted to? Examinations would be informal, personal, and subjective. The student might invite the teacher to assist with diagnosing the relative degree of mastery if such were important to the individual student. The purpose of testing is not for determination or justifying grades, nor is it to determine practical problem-solving skills. Instead it attempts to focus on personal development and the relative contribution made by what was experienced (learned) to the process of becoming or being.

Value Education

Idealism

For the idealist, teaching children values is basically the act of introducing them to the traditional values of their social group. These values are woven into the curriculum in literature, in history, in music, in art, in all areas possible. These tend to be imposed values which are backed up with rewards or punishments for acceptable and unacceptable performance. What this amounts to is an indoctrination of the young into the value structure of the parent society. Children are taught the difference between good-bad, right-wrong, and good-evil. Aesop's Fables are one example of idealist value education. Even in fairy tales good ultimately triumphs over evil. Plutarch's *Lives* provided models of life for the ancients.

Realism

The contemporary realist would probably handle value education by calling upon Piaget and Kohlberg and use what research says about stages of intellectual development and the process of learning moral behavior (moral development). Training in the norm values of the parent society, reinforced with behavioral psychology, is provided. Basically the norms are selected by adults from available research and taught to children and youth systematically, using concepts and techniques compatible with their levels of social, intellectual, and emotional development. The emphasis is on efficiently and economically training children in the acceptable behaviors in their social group.

Pragmatism

The pragmatist wants children to do more than hear about or read about values. The pragmatist teacher wants the child to experience values and to understand them at an experiential, practical, usable level. This is done through getting students actively involved in projects, simulation, and other student-produced evidence of learning. The pragmatist sees value education as a process that is lifelong and not as a thing to be "learned" in childhood. Important would be the exchange of ideas and discussion similar to the approach used in value clarification of Raths and Simon and the examination of the personal and social consequences of behavior discussed by Dewey. The teacher would introduce value topics (so could students) but there would not be the "right vs. wrong" of idealism or the "socially acceptable vs. unacceptable" of the realist. Pragmatist values cannot violate the democratic process, student involvement, or the practical impact on the society of the individual's actions.

Existentialism

For the existentialist value education is a matter of personal, individual choice, and it is going on lifelong. The individual is engaged in dialogue with the teacher and other "significant others" and is "encountering" values at a personal level in life, in art, in literature, in philosophy, and especially in personal existence. The teacher has a voice in the dialogue but does not have the power to dictate or punish because such behavior would abridge the individual's freedom to choose. There are no existential evangelists.

School as a Social Institution

Idealism

Idealists believe that school fulfills a significant function in human society in that it fulfills a spiritually necessary function. Idealists believe that in order to become truly "human," people need culture. Culture is best "delivered" through schooling or education. Schooling gives the individual a cultural birth as a spiritual and intellectual human being.

Realism

The realist believes that schooling fulfills a natural necessity in that human group life is preserved by education. Children become tamed or domesticated through school and also develop sophistication in society's

mores, folkways, rituals, and knowledge. Such sophistication is best achieved through schooling and since
there is so much to be learned in order for one to live
and function in complicated human society, it can be
best taught in an orderly, organized, systematic, natural fashion in school.

Pragmatism

The pragmatist assigns to school the task of reconstruction and improvement of individual and societal
experience. The school fulfills the role of teaching
children and youth how to function in life and in
society. The school's purpose is to imitate society and
life, so it must be related in form, structure, or content
to what society is like.

Existentialism

For existentialists, schools should provide experiences which meet the individual's needs for development
of selfhood and individual potential. The existentialist
suggests, somewhat tongue-in-cheek, that schools as
ordinarily constituted may meddle or interfere with the
lives and personal development of the students by sti-
fling individuality and personal freedom.

Play

Idealism

The idealist teacher would advocate and use a variety of kinds of play. The types of play would, however,
be adult-designed and -disciplined and would have set

rules and procedures for winning or playing. To idealists it is important to teach steps in their proper sequences. Idealist play would often have language associated with it, such as chanting and rhyming, and reason or logic would often be emphasized. There would be competition and winning and losing to build character and teach sportsmanship. Some play would be imitative of adult roles.

Realism

The realist would use materials developed from nature by adults to teach the desired lessons of nature through play. Adults would sequence and organize the play, and children and youth would be expected to learn and appreciate the natural order and hierarchy within games and play. Play would be out-of-doors where possible and would use "natural" toys. Children would be encouraged to play with toys such as sand piles and water tables if they could not use natural outdoor play areas.

Pragmatism

The pragmatist teacher would encourage play which emphasizes the group and social development of children. There would be a stress on cooperative and interactive play. The pragmatist would simulate social roles and encourage role playing. Where possible, play and work would be enjoyably combined so that worthwhile goals or products might be achieved.

Existentialism

In the view of the existentialist teacher, play serves

to further develop the selfhood of the learner. As such it should be unstructured and based on free child-choice. The creative visual or manipulative arts would be used. There would be variety and imagination used by the individual.

School Activities

Idealism

The co-curricular or extra-curricular activities of idealist schools consist of the traditional school clubs, organizations, and class activities, for example, honor societies, sodalities, scouts, retreats. They are strongly teacher-sponsor controlled and are primarily oriented to subject matter and accepted social, service, or religious functions. Sports are present but they are expected to develop character and contribute to building a strong body as a temple or housing for the mind. Social clubs are for manners and refinement. Honor societies and lettermen's clubs support the academic program and the scholar-athlete image.

Realism

Science and other academically-oriented clubs predominate in the realist schedule of school activities. They are under teacher-sponsor control. Scholastic honors or "letters" are important. Sports and sports clubs contribute to building strong bodies and strong minds. Most school activities are academically oriented. The early realist was interested in disciplining the body to the will of the mind.

Pragmatism

Pragmatist teachers advocate a school activities program that is multi-faceted and multi-purpose. There would be hobby clubs, sports, social clubs, student councils, student advisory groups, and academic clubs, each existing to meet individual needs and interests and also to provide social and leadership experiences for students outside of the classroom. Students get opportunities to practice doing and participating in non-classroom (real life) environments. Students are expected to provide leadership and membership, direction, and purpose, organization and management. Adults are the facilitators and the helpers; they are the guides and more experienced members.

Existentialism

For existentialists school activities exist only to serve the needs of the individual. They do not exist for themselves or to fulfill school traditions. Students provide direction based upon felt needs and choices. The activities would tend to be loosely and informally organized by students. Adults can help when they are asked or when they present ideas that are deemed relevant or meaningful to students.

School Buildings

Idealism

Idealists build school buildings that are basically traditional, that is, designed around single teacher-classroom spaces. They tend to be structured for one-way communication. Attractive auditoriums and stages are often a central focus in many buildings along with libraries and sometimes large lecture halls. Many classrooms have raised stages at one end which can be used for student recitation. The teacher's desk is often placed on this raised platform along with a lectern.

Realism

Realist school buildings are largely traditional, with enclosed, single-teacher classroom spaces. Science labs, rooms designed for media usage, and centralized media centers are often central features of realist schools. Realists are more media-oriented and their schools are somewhat more multi-purpose in scope than idealist schools, but they are still designed primarily for relatively passive student roles in which students react "on cue" and appropriately.

Pragmatism

The pragmatist school is designed for greater flexibility of use than idealist and realist buildings. There are flexible multi-purpose spaces which may be used for a variety of activities and with groups of different sizes. Movable walls, movable equipment, patios, and recreation spaces all increase the number of functions a school can serve. The manual and practical arts lab areas and classrooms with flexible space areas are often the center of attention in a pragmatist school.

Existentialism

Taking a lead from pragmatists, the existentialists would design a school building with a lot of open spaces and with open classrooms. The school would contain green spaces, soft spaces, informal spaces, large and small spaces, as well as more traditional spaces—all suited to a variety of modes and sizes of groups. Spaces for intimate dialogue and for student creativity would probably be some of the key features of the existential school.

School Climate

Idealism

The idealist wants the school climate to be contemplative, inspirational, studious, and formal. The school climate is to foster student mental activity in an adult-structured environment. Students are expected to be in passive and receptive modes of behavior.

Realism

The realist teacher wants a school which is business-like, orderly, efficient, and organized by the teacher. Activity is to be sequenced, sober, and serious. Like idealists, the realists encourage their version of mental activity in a controlled setting in which students seek the knowledge of the curriculum.

Pragmatism

The pragmatist prefers a school climate that is busy, active, social, flexible, and constructive. Students are to be involved in interactive processes on topics of practical or utilitarian concern. Although classrooms may have more movement and more noise than the idealist classroom, they should be constructive and self-controlled.

Existentialism

The existentialist would say that a climate of learning should be vital and alive, creative, reflective, individual, and open to opportunity. With dialogue or individual study or creation as the primary focus, one would expect such a climate to be quietly intense or conversationally noisy.

Classroom Design

Idealism

The central focus in the idealist classroom would be the teacher's desk. As noted previously, many idealist classrooms have a stage or a raised platform for presentations or recitations. Podiums or lecture stands also command a position of attention. Student furniture is usually sturdy and traditional and seating patterns are traditional and formal in a one-way communication design.

Realism

The central focus in the realist classroom would be the teacher demonstration (lab) table and the teaching station or lectern. There is likely to be a media station present in the realist classroom also (pictures, models, charts, mock-ups, aquariums, projectors, recorder-players, videos, etc.). Student seating is formal and teacher-controlled for maximum impact. Communication is one-way and open for student observation of demonstration, movies, lab specimens.

Pragmatism

The pragmatist classroom has diffused focus with flexible work spaces. It is less rigid and formal than the idealist or realist classroom. The emphasis is on multi-purpose spaces. Students select their seating and work patterns for interactive communication. The pragmatist classroom also utilizes learning centers for individual or small-group work.

Existentialism

Classrooms in existential schools would be arranged to liberate students from constriction and confinement through use of open spaces and an open classroom concept. Learning stations or study carrells of the student's choice would permit individualization. The classroom would allow for some semi-privacy, for informality, and for dialogue with a mixture of hard and soft, formal and informal, open and private spaces.

Leadership Training

Idealism

Idealists tend to be more interested in training leaders than in educating followers. The philosophy of leadership for idealism is rooted in either social class or in the aristocracy of intellect. Followers receive training in doing one's duty in conformity and obedience to duly designated authority.

Realism

Realists are elitists who advocate the training of leaders who, they contend, can be identified in school by their academic or intellectual capacity. The education of followers is not emphasized with any special curriculum or method.

Pragmatism

Pragmatists promote a democratic political system with opportunities for shared leadership through committees, councils, and wide grassroots participation. Followers are to be knowledgeable, capable, and able to step into leadership roles as occasions warrant. Pragmatists would say that different situations demand different abilities and different leadership skills and styles.

Existentialism

Existentialists contend that the individuality of all human beings is too important to groom only some for leadership and others as followers. The existentialist teacher would work to make all students leaders in the sense that all are capable of being responsible, sensitive, and thoughtful choice makers.

Motivation

Idealism

The idealist believes that the curriculum and the teacher are the chief sources of inspiration in the classroom. Rewards and punishments are motivational tools. Teacher charisma and persuasion are important. Idealists believe that the subject matter itself is exciting and motivating and that students should learn for the love of learning.

Realism

In realism the chief motivators are nature itself, which is viewed as intrinsically fascinating, and the expert technician-teacher, who uses organization and reinforcement to introduce students to nature and the sciences. Teachers try to keep their personalities out of their teaching. Appropriate use of classroom structure, material presentation, organization, sequencing, and reinforcement strategies manipulate student interest and activity.

Pragmatism

The pragmatist's chief motivator is to involve students in problem solving, in invention, and in creation. Student "ownership" or personal energy investment is considered to be intrinsically motivating. Learning by doing is exciting, and the process of participating, contributing, and interacting is the key. Teachers do use reinforcement to work on enhancement of self concept, and they try to capitalize on existing student interests by incorporating them into the classroom activities.

Existentialism

For the existentialist, personal relevance and meaningful creative activity are the only true motivators. The teacher should not try to manipulate the student's interest but identify and feed intrinsic student interest or desire, because the personhoods of both the teacher and the student are significant and not to be stifled or inhibited by artificial or arbitrary external influences.

Learning

Idealism

Idealist classrooms depend on mental activity that emphasizes memorization and imitative activity. Examples and worthy models are used extensively. Learning is almost always verbal or word-dependent. The concept of mental discipline, or doing difficult mental tasks to exercise the mind, is meaningful to idealists. They depend on the automatic transfer of knowledge and functions to new situations or new levels.

Realism

For realists, learning is seen basically as a bonding of stimulus and response. It is a behaviorist approach to the learning act. Laws of reinforcement and extinction are deliberately and carefully applied. Realists use a number of sensory modalities in instruction. The realist relies on structure and organization as tools of learning.

Pragmatism

Pragmatists define learning as a change in behavior resulting from experience(s) in which the learner is actively involved in thinking, solving problems, constructing, and reconstituting or reconstructing experiences. More socially valuable education results from such schooling, say the pragmatists. Learning is seen as a process. Teachers will utilize elements from both reinforcement behaviorist and gestalt or field theorists.

Existentialism

Learning is viewed by existentialists as mental and personal activity in which meaning is attached to that which is experienced as being relevant to the self.

Learning Theory

Idealism

Idealists depend on a traditional model of drill and theistic mental discipline. Faculty psychology is the basis of most idealist classroom practice in which the mental faculties are exercised and transfer is believed to occur automatically. Theorists include Saint Augustine, Plato, and J. Edwards.

Realism

Modern realists utilize stimulus-response bond/behaviorist theory, which is dependent upon conditioning, successive approximations, extinction theory, reinforcement schedules, and so on. Theorists include Thorndike, Hall, Skinner, Spence, Gagne, and Herbart.

Pragmatism

Pragmatists utilize some elements from reinforcement theory, Gestalt psychology, and field theory promoting insightful learning, continuity, and restructuring of experiences. Theorists include Lewin, Dewey, Combs, and Bandura.

Existentialism

Existential psychology of education is most clearly related to phenomenology. It includes elements of field theory and phenomenology with much attention to insightful learning and values. Theorists include Lewin and Rogers with interpretations by Maxine Green.

Teacher-Administration Relations

Idealism

In the idealist school the administrator is the highest authority. Teacher-administration relationships proceed on a superior/subordinate basis in which the superior may or may not be a benevolent master. Schools follow a traditional line and staff organization pattern, usually taking the format of an autocratic or military model tending toward "top down" communication.

Realism

In the realist school it is important to know who makes the decisions and who gives the orders. Realists are students of social structures. They develop line and staff flow charts similar to business organization models. Their organizational diagrams show lines of feedback, accountability lines, levels of authority, and clear indicators of responsibility.

Pragmatism

In pragmatist schools there is a good deal of commitment to group consensus and democratic process in the committees that develop policy. Administration shares responsibility and authority with teachers. The emphasis is on both social responsibility and individual rights. Basically it is a democratic model with an open-door policy and a faculty advisory or legislative council actively participating in administrative decision-making.

Existentialism

Existentialist school personnel have difficulty with traditional administrative structure because of the conflict which arises between being personally responsible and holding others responsible. There is a high degree of freedom for teachers to "do their own thing" and hold themselves responsible. Interaction between administrators and teachers is more similar to a persuasive dialogue between professional colleagues than anything else.

School Communications

Idealism

Idealist communications are formal and traditional: memos from the principal, formal faculty meetings, the use of titles, and staff newsletters. Communication is one-way, from top down, with the designated adults in charge. Staff and student formality and sponsor control of student publications are evident.

Realism

In realism there may be more concern for utilizing accepted (researched) communication models, but the formality exists and communication is basically adult-controlled and one-way. Memos from the principal are formal and functional, and so are faculty meetings.

Pragmatism

The communication format in the pragmatist school has less structure and more student involvement. There are staff newsletters, memos, student news-papers, and lots of faculty and student involvement in committees. An interactive communication pattern is followed. Meeting designs are informal and democratic and involve a lot of processing of information. Communication patterns are flexible to enhance speed, individual needs, and practical expediency.

Existentialism

School communication under existentialism depends on dialogue and one-to-one encounters. "Rap" sessions, discussions, and other informal designs are utilized. Much opportunity and encouragement exists for student-initiated communication and creative responses. Information flows freely among students, teachers, and administrators, and an atmosphere of openness prevails.

Budget Priorities

Idealism

Special budget allocations in idealist schools would probably be spent principally on books and materials to support the curriculum or the library and on bricks and mortar (because they last). Whatever can be done to support academics and excellence receives a high priority (especially in the humanities).

Realism

Realists allocate special funds according to established priorities, and here too they rely on one of a variety of business-type models. Higher priorities would ordinarily be given to supporting curricula in the sciences, math, and social sciences.

Pragmatism

For pragmatist educators the allocation of funds beyond subsistence is spread across the curriculum, but the highest priorities are given to practical arts, consumerism, vocational training, living skills, special education, etc. Each area gets its share (which would necessarily reduce the amount available for the humanities and the sciences).

Existentialism

Funding in existential schools is spent to foster creativity and individuality and programming in the performing and interpretive arts (drama, art, music, literature). There is some support for the basic humanities and philosophy because of their possible contribution to the search for self. Science and the practical courses would have a relatively low priority unless there was sufficient student interest manifested in them.

Creativity in School

Idealism

Student creativity in the idealist school is teacher-directed and teacher-judged. Creativity must meet external standards which emphasize originality but define it very traditionally. Creative efforts must be acceptable and avoid the radical. The expectation is that student creativity recreates what is already accepted as good or beautiful. How closely student efforts conform to known and accepted standards (the Masters) is the issue.

Realism

As in idealism, creativity in realism is teacher-directed and teacher-judged, but the standards are different, for although they are still external they reside in nature and in mastery of technique. There is little room for new or radical ideas without social norms for support. Creativity must imitate nature to be acceptable and to be judged beautiful.

Pragmatism

In pragmatist schools there is more concern for invention and for creative problem solving than for artistic creations because the mind is used constantly to put knowledge into new combinations and to invent and create new concepts. Judgment is based on questions such as: "Does it work?" "Is it useful or efficient?" The standards are situationally determined and flexible. There can be shared or group creative efforts. Pragmatist creativity in schools is inventive rather than "re-creative" or "imitative."

Existentialism

In existentialist schools the individual's creation of his or her self is the most important thing. Creativity is sought. Expression of selfhood is also significant. There are few (if any) rules of measurement. The critic or external judgment according to standards is unimportant. The key concept is individual creativity.

Textbooks

Idealism

Idealist schools believe that original sources (preferably neither translated nor paraphrased) are the best books available. Reading is a significant learning avenue and books are very important. It is preferred that there is little or no art work or charts or pictures supporting the text. Words are considered sufficient. Textbooks and library books are the important repositories of truth.

Realism

Realist texts contain logical, sequential, scientifically-developed material. They result from research.

There are pictures, charts, and graphs to support the text material. The realists were the first to illustrate texts (J. A. Comenius, *Orbus Pictus*). The text is the curriculum, and it represents nature and reality.

Pragmatism

In pragmatist classrooms, texts and other books are tools to be used by the individual to make sense out of one's own world. Books are illustrated for practical and utilitarian assistance to the reader. Other media can be of equal importance. Experience (direct or vicarious) can be as important as the printed word.

Existentialism

For existentialists the library may be more important than the textbook. But, of course, it is the meaning that the student attaches to the concepts that is most important. Words by themselves have no meaning.

Grade Level and Subject Organization

Idealism

Idealists adhere rather rigidly to grade-level organization (grade placement by age) and a traditional approach to subject matter organization. There is a reliance upon the way things have been done in the past. Courses are organized along the curriculum priorities mentioned earlier, that is, separated into discrete grades and classes with a narrow focus in each subject taught.

Realism

Realists make a serious attempt to analyze and sequence the subject matter from grade level to grade level. There is a firm adherence to the grade-by-grade sequence of subjects to be followed by students. Realists would introduce systematic training in science and scientific methodology as well as higher math earlier in a child's schooling than the other philosophies would. For additional realist subject organization see the section on curriculum priorities.

Pragmatism

Pragmatists are not so rigidly bound to a lock-step organization of curriculum as their idealist and realist counterparts. Because student social development is also important to pragmatists, an effort is made to integrate students with their social peers as well as their age mates and those with similar academic ability. In courses focusing on problem-solving, material is pulled from several discrete fields of study to be utilized in solving practical life-oriented problems. The pragmatists have also pioneered in non-graded instructional organization.

Existentialism

The existentialist tries hard to break the typical lock-step approach to school organization by abandoning traditional school patterns. Open schools, open classrooms, individualization of instruction, individual progress, non-competitive grading, and non-graded schools are designed to promote individuality.

Use of Technology

Idealism

Idealists would make only a limited use of technology and then primarily to supplement lecture or bring "classics" into the classroom. The personality and the impact of the teacher (lecturer) is too important to lose. Simple programmed instruction as a homework resource is acceptable. Some contemporary Christian academies are solving pupil-teacher ratio problems and dealing with control issues by using carefully written "Christian-oriented" programmed instruction within the classroom.

Realism

In the classroom, realists make a fairly broad application of technology and media to enhance nature's role and to promote science. Programmed instruction, media, lab materials and other kinds of aids are welcomed as an enhancement of the teacher's planning and organization. They are carefully coordinated with other methods for maximum student impact.

Pragmatism

Pragmatists consider the use of technology by teachers and students as a means of enhancing the processes of problem-solving. "It it works, use it." Such is the attitude of most pragmatists (especially if it works better, is more economical with similar results, or saves time). In pragmatist classrooms, it is usually the students who select and utilize the media in their studies or in the reports and presentations that they make to classmates.

Existentialism

Existentialists are somewhat skeptical of technology and fads and are reluctant to use them except to supplement the teacher's role to permit and enhance student development and creativity.

Innovation

Idealism

The idealist is skeptical of any change which threatens "time honored" methods, curriculum, and roles. Unless it serves some highly valued purpose, innovation is avoided.

Realism

Realists are willing to accept innovation if it has been adequately tested to validate its contribution. The testing that innovation must withstand is rigorous and time-consuming. Innovations within these limits are acceptable.

Pragmatism

The pragmatist uses innovation (or any other method that works) to enhance learning, personal growth, and problem-solving. The pragmatist is constantly on the search for new ways of achieving worthwhile goals more efficiently. Relativism, acceptance of change, and reconstruction of experience all set a climate that promotes innovation.

Existentialism

Since personal meaning and relevance are the key for existentialists, flux, innovation, and change are relatively easy for them to accept. The existentialist is no slave to accepting innovation, for that would be conformity. The existentialist must choose and select carefully from among available alternatives.

Attitude toward Humanism

Idealism

Idealists oppose modern humanism on the grounds that it dilutes the rigors of the traditional curriculum and it does not teach time-tested moral values. The humanist emphasis on individuality and independent thought is rejected, especially for children and youth, for it leads to the erosion of moral fiber. Fundamental idealists sometimes consider advocates of the other three philosophies to be "godless" secular humanists because of their doubts concerning acceptance of idealist truths and values.

Realism

To the realist, the whole question of humanism as viewed by the idealist is simply not relevant, for realists see the individual as part of nature and subject to the laws and interactions of nature. Humans are rational animals obligated to use their intellect to look beyond the obvious. It is profitable to spend time pursuing academically sound understanding of human beings, of the environment, and of the laws governing the physical and socio-political universe (thus developing intellect and rational power). The realist movement in the 18th and 19th centuries helped give birth to "classical humanism," which is probably one of the ancestors of modern humanism.

Pragmatism

Modern humanism is acceptable to the pragmatist as long as the individual's responsibilities are developed in a social or political context. As individuality and independence of thought are fostered, the goal must be that of improving the lot of all or showing one how to resolve social or interpersonal problems. Generally, the concept of humanism is acceptable as long as it can contribute to the improvement of the individual and the society.

Existentialism

Modern humanism is compatible with the existentialist emphasis on individuality and independence of thought and action. Individual meaning and relevance are key issues to understanding the existentialist's endorsement of humanism.

Library or Media Center

Idealism

To the idealist the library is the heart of the school. It

is the embodiment of timeless wisdom and the storehouse of culture, tradition, and civilization. Books and printed material are the most important elements in the idealist library. Non-print materials would most likely be reproductions of approved masterworks of idealist art.

Realism

The media center is important to realists because it contains the curriculum of nature and the means by which to understand it. As in idealism, the media center may well be the most important room in the school. Non-print materials of a variety of kinds including audio-visual technology are also available there.

Pragmatism

To the pragmatist the media center is a huge tool kit to be used by students and faculty to understand their environment and to solve their problems. Subscriptions to current periodicals, newspapers, and other sources covering contemporary issues would receive priority. So too would the sections of the collection dealing with practical subjects and vocational or career education. There is also some likelihood that, in the effort to make the library really usable, parts of its collection might be located in classrooms.

Existentialism

Existentialists accept interacting with books and media as being important, but state clearly that first-hand human encounter with life's drama and difficulty is the most important element. Classroom collections to enhance student involvement with literature and art depicting the human dilemma and absurdity would be advocated. The existentialist library would be rather untraditional in its collection, its checkout practices, and in the way it would be managed.

Role of the Counselor

Idealism

The idealist defines the counselor more as a mentor or dean of students who gives sound advice on moral and academic matters. The counselor operates as the older, more experienced adult telling students what they need to know and what they ought to do. The counselor's job is to turn young people into the adults they ought to be.

Realism

The realists define the counselor as a guidance worker, as a giver of tests, and a compiler of data for sound decision-making based on norms and standards. The counselor is a recommender of courses of action and academic programs. Their recommendations are based upon test results, numerical data and other available student information. There is concern for conformity to norm groups, and it is important to identify the square pegs and match them up with square holes of appropriate sizes.

Pragmatism

The pragmatist counselor applies data practically

and individually. In more specific terms, the counselor is a problem solver and works with clients to identify (diagnose) and resolve personal and social problems. The pragmatist counselor tries to explore personal and social implications of actions and decisions and is interested in analyzing personal and social environments and the interactions of individuals within them. This counselor is trying to help pegs of different shapes find the holes best suited to them.

Existentialism

The existentialist is a non-directive counselor listening and reflecting while the clients (students) try to attach meaning to their individual life events. The purpose of counseling is to help clients hear what they are saying and to discover meaning in their personal life dilemmas and to define themselves. The counselor-client relationship is one-to-one and proceeds principally as a reflective dialogue in which the pegs find holes of their own choosing.

The Counselor's Use of Groups

Idealism

The idealist counselor makes presentations to large groups of students to give them instruction and information. At times, mentor/disciple relationships are developed in very small groups or individually.

Realism

Realist counselors fulfill the guidance function mainly by presenting information to large groups.

They do, however, tend to work one-to-one in the application and the interpretation of data.

Pragmatism

Pragmatist counselors make extensive use of a variety of groups of different sizes for varied tasks. They use large-group interactions (not just lecturing), medium and small groups, role playing, socio-drama, and they also counsel one-to-one.

Existentialism

Because dialogue is best conducted in intimate settings, the existentialist works principally one-to-one, and if groups are used at all, they are very small.

Counselor Use of Tests

Idealism

Idealists avoid the use of standardized tests for they believe that a student's previous academic record is the best predictor of his or her future success.

Realism

The realist relies heavily on standardized testing and normed data as the basis for counseling. Both individual and group tests are used.

Pragmatism

The pragmatist believes that both social and academic performance are important. There is also appropriate use of tests for individual analysis and diagnosis to assist students in reaching competence and mastery in both areas of performance.

Existentialism

For the existentialist, impersonal tests with obvious flaws and cultural biases are less important than what can be learned and exchanged in face-to-face encounters.

Counseling Models

Idealism

The idealist is most likely to utilize a pastoral counseling model such as that advocated by J. E. Adams, who sees a counselor as an older and wiser representative of culture (or super force) giving good advice to the client on how to live the good life.

Realism

The realist is indebted for his or her counseling models to such theorists as E. G. Williamson and the more contemporary behaviorists such as B. F. Skinner, both of whom define counselors either as guidance workers making sound data-based recommendations or as behaviorist engineers helping to reshape behavior.

Pragmatism

The pragmatist counselor owes allegiance to theorists such as Krumboltz and Glasser. They also make use of sociometry (a la Bonney or Fessendon). The classroom (or group counseling setting) is a society in miniature and all students have a voice there and the right to emotional, psychological, and physical protection from harassment. The individuals can solve problems and give mutual support and challenge in a democratic setting.

Existentialism

The existentialists are most likely to utilize the counseling model promoted by Carl Rogers or the phenomenologists in which counselors operate non-directively and reflect the client's feelings and thoughts back to them so that the meanings can be examined in intimate one-to-one encounters.

Educational Theorists and Models

Idealism

The idealists rely on a variety of educational models and theorists although there are common threads that run through them. The most likely school model to be followed would be a traditional parochial prep school design. The theorists would range from Plato to Hegel, Herman Horne to W.T. Harris. The Jesuits and Pope Pius XI also provide strong idealist educational models.

Realism

The realist educational theorists and models are Aristotle, Herbert Spencer, J. F. Herbart, Comenius, John Locke, F. Bacon, Ralph B. Perry, and Harry

Broudy. The primary models are provided by behavioral educational psychologists and by the Soviet school model.

(Essentialism is an integration of educational, curricular, and methodological elements of both realism and idealism. Essentialism has many advocates but none are more significant than W. C. Bagley and Frederick Breed.)

Pragmatism

The pragmatist educator draws upon theorists beginning with Quintillian and extending to John Dewey, W. H. Kilpatrick, Ernest Bayles, Boyd Bode, and Sidney Hook. The primary model of the modern pragmatist school would be the comprehensive high school.

(Progressive education owes a debt to both realism and pragmatism, with Francis Parker, Froebel, and Montessori providing historical parentage along with Dewey and others.)

Existentialism

The existentialist educator relies upon A. S. Neill and Maxine Greene as theorists, and the principal school model is the Summerhill School and some of the Free School experiments of the 1960's.

Review Chart
for Philosophies and Topics

Topics	Idealism	Realism	Pragmatism	Existentialism
	Outside of humans Absolute	Outside of humans Absolute	Function of interaction of experience and intellect	Individually determined
Truth	Discovered Mental/spiritual Super force	Discovered Natural universe Observation/science	Relative Practical	Personal meaning Based on choices and actions
Value	Apart from humans Eternal Discovered Super force	Apart from humans Natural Discovered (observed) Norms/standards	Social interaction created by humans Practical/useful Use of intellect	Individually and relatively based on choice
Nature of Human Being	Super force's creation Spiritual/mental Passive Either good or bad	Creature of nature Rational animal Reactive Good in natural state	Bio-socio-psycho individuals Inventive/adapting Interactive Neutral	Potential Defining Self Rational/irrational Transactional Choosers

Topics	Idealism	Realism	Pragmatism	Existentialism
Good Life	Harmony with super force Spiritual/mental excellence Service/sacrifice	Harmony with nature/society Mental development Science/observation	Harmony with self/society Useful/practical Political/social Individual experience	Harmony with self Full self-development Choice/freedom Authenticity
Tradition	History is important Tradition is vital Based in superforce	Reject idealist tradition Science/observation Based in nature	Examine all tradition Practicality and utility are more important	Individual meaning is more important than tradition Nonconformity Freedom
Freedom	Within limits Conform to ideal Subordinate to super force Free will (?)	Within limits set by nature Free within norms Nature/nurture Rational	Socio-political context sets limits Democracy Free will and responsibility	Humans exist Total freedom Consequences

Topics	Idealism	Realism	Pragmatism	Existentialism
Creativity	Super force is the creator Glorify super force Religious/nationalist themes	Nature is creative and evolutionary Emphasis on technique Genetic gift	Individual mind invents/creates Reconstruction of experience Social context	Personal Creation of self Authenticity Abstract/feeling
Power	From super force To be used for good Glorify super force	From nature Learn to use nature's power Knowledge is power	Interaction of individuals in social settings Individuals have power	Personal power of choice/action Use for authenticity Individual responsibility
Morality	Dependent upon super force Tradition Absolutes	Dependent upon nature Norms/standards Social origins	Dependent upon social interaction Practical Democratic Human rights	Dependent on individual Needs Choices Consequences

Topics	Idealism	Realism	Pragmatism	Existentialism
Decision-making	Will of super force Traditions tell how "at one with" super force	Accordance with nature Conform to natural law "At one with" nature	Practical/useful Social/political Non-conformist	Individual choice Nontraditional Total personal responsibility
Love	From super force Traditional models Altruism	Physical/genetic Learned behavior Conservation	Social interaction Learned behavior Service to society	Personal development Individual as chooser Love of self
Future	Controlled by super force History revealing itself Fate/pre-destination Closed system	Evolving naturally Sciences for prediction Determinism Closed system	Planned by human beings Adapting/adopting Change is constant Open system	In hands of the individual Choices create the future Open system

Topics	Idealism	Realism	Pragmatism	Existentialism
Change	History and tradition change little if at all. Super force controls change	Nature is evolving within a plan. Change is inevitable	Progress. Relativity. Process. Ongoing change	Constant human definition of self in choice. Accepted
Culture	Creation of super force. Civilizing agent. Traditional	By-product of society. Culture may corrupt youth	Created by people. Product of socialization and experience	Individual created by self. Personal relevance

Topics	Idealism	Realism	Pragmatism	Existentialism
Representative philosophers	St. Augustine Bogoslovsky, B.B. Butler, J. Donald Demiashkevitch Fairbairn, A.M. Gentile, Giovanni Hegel, G.W.F. Hocking, William Horne, Herman H. Kant, Immanuel Plato Royce, Josiah	Aristotle St. Thomas Aquinas Breed, F.S. Broudy, Harry Comenius, John Amos Descartes, Rene Herbert, J.F Locke, John Perry, R.B. Rousseau, J.J. (naturalism) Whitehead, A.N.	Bayles, E.E. Berkson, I.B. Bode, Boyd H. Brameld, Theodore (reconstruction) Childs, John Dewey, John Hook, Sidney James, William Kilpatrick, William, H. Peirce, C.S.	Barrett, William Buber, Martin Heidegger, Martin Jaspers, Karl Kierkegaard, S. Morris, Van Cleve Nietzsche, F. Sartre, Jean Paul Teilhard de Chardin, Pierre Tillich, Paul

Review Chart
for
Educational Issues and Topics

Topics	Idealism	Realism	Pragmatism	Existentialism
Purpose of education	Prepare for adulthood Conform to super force	Prepare for adulthood Conform to nature	Become socially valuable person now and later Learn how to learn	Become authentic Encourage selfhood
Curriculum	Liberal arts Humanities The "trivium"	Science, math, social science The "quadrivium"	Social studies Practical arts Problem-solving	Fine arts Creative expression Human dilemma
Curricular Emphasis	Cognitive Knowledge Skills with words	Cognitive Knowledge Skills with science	Cognitive/affective Knowledge/process Attitudes	Affective Individual Self-development Skills with thinking
Approach to subject matter	Structured Rigid curriculum Pre-existent reality	Structured Rigid curriculum External reality	Amorphous Flexible curriculum Process oriented Social needs	Amorphous Individual curriculum Personal needs

Topics	Idealism	Realism	Pragmatism	Existentialism
Subject matter and knowledge	Finite Known to super force Revealed	Objective Natural Science/observation	Created and used Social/personal Process	Personal creation Self-relevant Various sources
Role of the teacher	Model of morality and scholarship Mentor Charismatic	Model of science and scholarship Mentor Conduit	Participant Facilitator Example of problem solver	Fellow searcher Questioner Half of a dialogue
Methods of instruction	Lecture Recitation Essays Word dependent	Lecture Recitation Labs/audiovisual Words and things	Problem solving Activity Group work Discussion	Individual Dialogue Encounter Creation
Agent of change	Learn time-tested Preserve status quo Traditions	Test and verify Evolution in nature is slow Order	Processes Change/flux Alternatives Practicality	Individual change Allowed but not provoked

Topics	Idealism	Realism	Pragmatism	Existentialism
Permanence and change	Abolute-ism Permanence Tradition	Absolute-ism Natural evolution Tested	Relativism Change is the only constant	Personalism Flexibility Freedom
Teacher's power roles	Traditional Adults know, children do not Exemplar of the ideal	Traditional Authoritarian Exemplar of nature	Democratic Non-authoritarian Guide	Individual choice Non-authoritarian Co-equals
School rules	Traditional Time-tested Adults	Traditional Norm-tested Adults	Contemporary Democratic Negotiated	Individual responsibility
Learner expectation	Obedience Scholarship Conformity Little adults	Obedience Scholarship Conforming Little animals	Participation Curiosity Ownership Experiencing	Questioning Creative Responsible Free

Topics	Idealism	Realism	Pragmatism	Existentialism
Preferred student role	Traditional Passive Obedient Receiver	Natural Reactive Obedient Responder	Participant Interactive Responsible Initiator	Active Curious Developing Creator
Individual difference	No individualization Students conform to expectations	Tracking Students conform to norms	Individualized Small groups Student needs	Individual choice and activity
Individual rights	Traditional definitions Super force comes first Elitism	Social norms for definitions Part of nature	Democratic Responsible Equality	Individual freedom Responsible Consequences
Discipline expectations	Obedience Mental discipline Rules/punishments Extrinsic/adults	Behaviorism Modification Reinforcement Extrinsic/adults	Negotiation Participation Ownership Interactive	Individual Internal Consequences Intrinsic

Topics	Idealism	Realism	Pragmatism	Existentialism
Play	Adult-designed Adult-directed Formal/rules Character building	Natural materials Adult-organized Out of doors Real/simulation	Teacher/facilitators Group/social Cooperative Interactive	Unstructured Free play Creative Variety/imagination
Discipline models	"Spare the rod, spoil the child" Rewards/punishments "Tough love" Corporal punishment James Dobson	Behavior modification Reinforcement schedule Extinction Assertive discipline Skinner, Canter	Natural consequences Democratic Student involvement Ownership Driekurs, Dewey	Individual meaning Consequences Responsibility A.S. Neill
Special student needs	Academic talent All must meet "the standards" Push bright kids	Academic talent Tracking in the basic curriculum Some special education	Individual needs Vocational life oriented classes Variety Special education and mainstreaming	Complete individualization to meet needs

Topics	Idealism	Realism	Pragmatism	Existentialism
Type of thinking prized	Rote memory Traditional Convergent Inductive Aristotelian logic	Memorization of structures/ principles Divergent Scientific Deductive	Problem-solving Alternatives Students involved Divergent Experimental	Individual Divergent Creative Alternatives Abstract-personal
Who has knowledge	Books Schools Teachers Adults	Books Schools Teachers Adults	Thinking people (including children) Learning is a process	Children can know and attach meaning Independent learning
Who is in charge of the learning space	High teacher control Low student control	High teacher control Low student control	Equality Parity Shared control	High student control Low teacher control
Classroom center	Curriculum-centered Teacher-centered	Curriculum-centered Teacher-centered	Process-centered Child-centered Activity-centered Shared/ relational	Person-centered Emerging-student-centered

Topics	Idealism	Realism	Pragmatism	Existentialism
Accountability	To excellence To academics Traditional Liberal arts model	To excellence To society Statistics/norms Standardized testing	Society and to the individual Tests for diagnosis Social improvements	To selfhood To authenticity
Teaching: art or science?	Teaching, especially lecturing, is an art form	Scientific Organized Technical (Herbartian)	Interactive process with both technical skills and artistry	Art form (probably a duet) Dialogue Encounter
Objectives	Classical/ traditional Adult-selected Broad teacher goals	Objective/ scientific Adult-selected Specific Behavioral	Jointly-selected Renegotiable Mutual	Student-selected Individual choice

Topics	Idealism	Realism	Pragmatism	Existentialism
Back to basics	Tool subjects Humanities Liberal arts Higher standards	Tool subjects Math, science Social sciences Higher standards	Tool subjects Social studies Consumer/vocational Practical Meet needs	Tool subjects Living skill Arts/humanities Personal adjustment Individual meaning
Examinations and testing	Essays Teacher-judged Formal External standards	Objective Standardized Lab performance External standards	Practical Application Hands-on Some group work Problem-solving	Dialogue (oral) Self evaluation Student-produced work
Value education	Imposed Moral training Indoctrination Rewards/punishments	Moral development Social training Reinforcement	Idea exchange Value clarification Personal/social consequences	Dialogue Personal value Choice

Topics	Idealism	Realism	Pragmatism	Existentialism
School as a social institution	Spiritual necessity Cultural birth Man needs culture	Natural necessity Group life is preserved Respect nature	Imitates life How to function Improves individuals	Individual development Authentic selfhood
School activities	Traditional Teacher-controlled Support academics Build character	Subject clubs Teacher controlled Academic orientation Cost-effective	Multi-faceted Multi-purpose Social development Student-controlled	Serve individual needs only
School buildings	Traditional Enclosed spaces Single teacher Inflexible One-way	Largely traditional Enclosed spaces Single teacher Media applicable Passive students	Flexible Multi-purpose Group work Team teaching Interactive	Open space Informal Varied uses

Topics	Idealism	Realism	Pragmatism	Existentialism
School climate	Contemplative Formal Studious Inspirational	Businesslike Organized Sequenced	Busy Practical Social Interactive	Vital Creative Individual Open
Classroom design	Central focus— teacher stations Recitation stage Traditional seating One-way	Central focus— demonstra- tion table, lectern Media usage Observation	Diffuse focus Flexible Learning centers Informal seat- ing Two-way	Open concept Open space Informal Dialogue
Leadership training	Elitist Social class Intellect	Elitist Intellect	Democratic (shared)	Individual
Sources of motivation	Curriculum Teacher personality Rewards/pun- ishments	Curriculum Teacher organization Reinforcement	Activity Involvement Social group Experience Student needs	Personal relevance Activity Creation

Topics	Idealism	Realism	Pragmatism	Existentialism
Learning	Mental discipline Rote memory Imitative Automatic transfer	Stimulus-response Behaviorism Reinforcement Extinction	Change behavior Active Student needs	Mental Personal Meaningful
Learning models	Traditional drill Theistic mental discipline Faculty psychology St. Augustine, Plato, J. Edwards	Stimulus-response Behaviorist Conditioning Reinforcement Hull, Thorndike, Skinner, Spence, Gagne, Herbart	S-R/Gestalt Field theory Insight Lewin, Dewey, Combs, Bandura	Phenomenology Consciousness Insights Valences Lewin, Rogers
Teacher and administration relations	Line/staff model Authoritarian Formal Military model	Line/staff model Executive Formal Business model	Committee model Shared authority Informal Democratic model	Individual Persuasion Informal Dialogue

Topics	Idealism	Realism	Pragmatism	Existentialism
School communications	Formal Traditional One-way Adult-controlled	Formal Functional One-way Adult-controlled	Less structured Interactive Process-oriented Students involved	Informal Dialogue Open Student-initiated
School policy	Authority-centered Chain of command Unchangeable	Leader-centered Flow charts Slow change	Democratic Process/interactive Negotiation	Consensus Informed discourse Changeable
Budget allocation	Bricks/mortar Support academics Humanities Library	Priorities chosen Support academics Science/math Media	Comprehensive Support practical subjects Social development Individual development	Creativity Creative arts Humanities Individual

Topics	Idealism	Realism	Pragmatism	Existentialism
Creativity in school	Teacher-controlled Teacher-judged External standards Re-creative	Teacher-controlled Teacher-judged External standards Imitative	Individual Problem-solving Workability Inventive	Individual Expression of selfhood Creative
Grade level and subject organization	Rigid adherence to grade level Formal Traditional	Rigid adherence to grade level Traditional Structured Sequenced approach	Non-graded Social development Problem-centered Informal	Nonconformist Open classroom Personal Informal
Textbooks	Original sources Word dependent Reading to get the truth of super force	Scientific development Visuals to support text Represents nature	Tools to be used Equal to media or other sources Supports experience	Words (books) have no meaning by themselves

Topics	Idealism	Realism	Pragmatism	Existentialism
Library and media center	Library is central Embodies the curriculum Books Traditional	Media center focus Contains nature Books/media	Media center is a tool to be used Understand one's environment Decentralized	Books and media may help to understand the human dilemma Classroom collections
Attitude toward modern humanism	Opposed to it No moral values Non-traditional Too much freedom "secular humanists"	Not relevant Subject to nature Develop the mind Deemphasized the individual	Acceptable Social/political Individual and society Social improvement	Compatible Individual Choice making Relevance Self development
Use of technology	Restricted Threat to the personality of the lecturer	Broad application Enhance nature Media usage	Utilitarian Problem-solving Application of knowledge	Skeptical Dialogue Encounter Enhance creativity

Topics	Idealism	Realism	Pragmatism	Existentialism
Innovation	Skeptical Threat to tradition Difficult to promote	Qualified Validated Rigorous tests Within limits	Enhance learning Alternatives Workability Experience	Nonconformist Personal Relevant Consequences
Role of the counselor	Mentor Dean of students Advisor	Guidance worker Psychometrist Interpreter	Problem solver Facilitator Analyzer	Non-directive Clarifier Reflector
Counselor use of groups	Large group Counselor-led One-to-one	Large group Counselor-led One-to-one	Variety of sizes Student-led Shared responsiblity	Small groups Pairs/dialogue Intimate
Counselor use of tests, records, and data	Academic record	Standardized Normed tests	Social and academic performance Some testing	Little testing Dialogue

Topics	Idealism	Realism	Pragmatism	Existentialism
Counseling models	Pastoral counseling J.E. Adams	E.G. Williamson B.F. Skinner Behaviorists	Krumboltz Glasser	Rogers Phenomenologists
Educational models	Plato, Jesuits, Pope Pius XI (1929), Hegel, H. Horne, W.T. Harris, Traditional parochial prep school model	Aristotle, H. Spencer, J.F. Herbart, Comenius, J. Locke, H. Broudy, F. Froebel, Soviet school model	Quintillian, John Dewey, W.H. Kilpatrick, E.E. Bayles, B. Bode, Sidney Hook, Comprehensive high school models	A.S. Neill, Maxine Greene, Summerhill School model Free schools (1960's)
		Essentialism W.C. Bagley, Frederick Breed	Progressivism Francis Parker, M. Montessori	

Review Test

This section contains multiple choice questions that will help the student test his or her understanding of the principles and applications of the four philosophies of education addressed in this book: idealism, realism, pragmatism, and existentialism. Following the questions is an answer key.

The review test is divided into two parts. Part I covers the four philosophies as they relate to the abstract topics (e.g., truth, value, freedom, love, etc.) introduced in Section I of this book. A set of four questions is presented under each of these topics.

In Part II of the review test the questions are focused on the four philosophies as they apply to the educational issues and topics covered in Section II. No topic headings are provided in the second part of the review test. Students may wish to pencil-check their answer choices in the margin or write them on a separate piece of paper.

Part I. The Four Philosophies
As They Relate to Abstract Topics

Truth

1. The idea that truth is mental and spiritual is most closely associated with
   A. realism
   B. idealism
   C. pragmatism
   D. existentialism
2. Realists contend that truth may be found in
   A. Plato's world of ideas
   B. the personal meaning of things
   C. nature and the laws governing its elements
   D. the interaction of the human intellect with the environment
3. For pragmatists, truth is
   A. changeable
   B. absolute and eternal
   C. personal
   D. universal
4. Existentialists would say that truth is
   A. absolute and eternal
   B. a matter of personal interpretation
   C. revealed in the writing of great thinkers and prophets
   D. a function of the human intellect interacting with the environment

Value

5. According to realists, values are derived from
   A. reading the documents of learned men
   B. determining what is practical and useful
   C. studying nature
   D. striving to be authentic

6. That each person creates his or her own values through choosing and acting would be consistent with the thinking of
   A. pragmatists
   B. realists
   C. idealists
   D. existentialists

7. Values are created as a result of social human interactions, according to
   A. idealists
   B. realists
   C. pragmatists
   D. existentialists

8. Values do not change over time because the truths to which they relate do not change. Those who agree with this statement are probably
   A. idealists
   B. realists
   C. existentialists
   D. pragmatists

Nature of the Human Being

9. Idealists believe that human beings are
   A. creatures of nature and part of the natural order
   B. basically neutral with the capacity to learn to be good or bad, as defined by society

C. potential in motion and in the process of defining themselves.

D. basically passive and subject to the will of a superior power

10. The belief that we as human beings are "the sum total of our experiences" is most closely associated with

A. idealism

B. realism

C. pragmatism

D. existentialism

11. The pragmatist would describe human beings as

A. biological, social, psychological organisms in which those three functions are continuously interacting

B. thinking, feeling, choosing beings who are responsible for the consequences of their decisions

C. organisms at the top of the evolutionary ladder

D. spiritual and mental beings who are part of a grand plan

12. Human beings are viewed as being transactional internally and socially by

A. idealists

B. realists

C. pragmatists

D. existentialists

The Good Life

13. Achieving one's potential and choosing to become a genuine being is a fundamental goal of

A. pragmatists
B. idealists
C. existentialists
D. realists

14. Pragmatists believe that one measure of the good life is whether or not one is
A. living in harmony with the laws of nature
B. living in harmony with society
C. achieving one's individual potential
D. growing spiritually

15. The good life for realists consists of
A. useful, practical, social, and political action in behalf of society
B. astute observation and scholarly investigation with the goal of achieving congruity with nature and its laws
C. choosing and acting in authentic ways
D. developing one's spiritual and mental capacities in keeping with traditional teachings

16. For the idealist the good life is defined by
A. pursuing excellence and academics and living a life of sacrifice and service to forces greater than the individual
B. reaching a state of harmony with nature and the physical laws of the universe
C. committing one's self to democratic principles and processes
D. achieving one's potential

Tradition

17. To existentialists, reliance upon conformity to tradition would be
A. useful in the development of the individual life

B.   in conflict with existential thought
C.   acceptable in some instances
D.   none of the above

18.   Any traditions that realists would accept would have to
A.   encourage personal freedom and development of the self
B.   be useful and practical in contemporary society
C.   be based in scientology
D.   be supported by scientific investigation and natural laws

19.   Pragmatists would agree that traditions have validity so long as they are
A.   properly respected and portrayed
B.   rooted in science and natural law
C.   contributing to the success of democratic social processes
D.   based on scholarly documents from the past

20.   History and the past are most basic to the philosophy of
A.   idealism
B.   realism
C.   pragmatism
D.   existentialism

Freedom

21.   The exercise of free choice within the limitations set by nature and natural law is a concept of freedom that would be supported by
A.   pragmatists
B.   idealists
C.   realists

D. existentialists

22. What is legal, reasonable, and good for the development of society would be a condition of freedom for
A. pragmatists
B. idealists
C. realists
D. existentialists

23. Traditions, rituals, and rules have an important bearing on one's freedom, according to
A. pragmatists
B. idealists
C. realists
D. existentialists

24. On the subject of freedom, existentialists would say that
A. it is the capacity to think and create within a social-political context of democracy
B. human freedom is limited by the fact that people are subordinate to the laws of nature
C. human beings individually are free to develop or create themselves and to give meaning to their existence
D. the notion of free will should be rejected

Creativity

25. Portrayals of sacrifice, reverence, and martyrdom are seen often in the fine art produced by
A. existentialists
B. pragmatists
C. realists
D. idealists

26. A dominant theme in existential art is
A. one of denial of self

    B.   human absurdity

    C.   nature

    D.   progress

27.   Creative efforts in the fine arts which are valued highly by realists are those that

    A.   have a religious or nationalistic theme

    B.   tend toward the abstract and have personal meaning to the artist

    C.   imitate and portray nature in its unspoiled form

    D.   focus on themes such as progress, evolution, and social interaction

28.   The inventiveness of a writer, artist, or musician is a feature that would be most highly appreciated by

    A.   idealists

    B.   realists

    C.   pragmatists

    D.   existentialists

Power

29.   An existentialist would contend that power should be used for

    A.   improving society

    B.   achieving harmony with nature

    C.   protecting a nation's way of life

    D.   fulfilling one's potential

30.   Where power is concerned, idealists would tend to support the theory that

    A.   all humans have it and are totally responsible for how they use it

    B.   it can be achieved by learning to control and use nature

C. it arises as a result of human interaction in social environments

D. some classes, nations, or families are meant to have more of it than others

31. As one develops knowledge of the universe and its laws, one also develops power, according to

A. idealists
B. realists
C. pragmatists
D. existentialists

32. Those who believe that individuals have power inherently but should surrender it to others for social and political progress are probably

A. idealists
B. realists
C. pragmatists
D. existentialists

Morality

33. Internal personal harmony with the self is an important element of morality for

A. the idealist
B. the realist
C. the pragmatist
D. the existentialist

34. For pragmatists, moral codes are best derived from

A. the needs and aspirations of individuals and social groups
B. studies by social scientists
C. traditions and laws of long standing
D. nature and natural law

35. For idealists, morality is best defined and supported by

    A.   nature and natural law
    B.   tradition
    C.   the self
    D.   society's needs

36.   Realists would argue that morality must be based on
    A.   principles that have their origin in the past
    B.   what is deemed to be moral by the society at large at any given time based on scientific investigation
    C.   society's preference expressed in a vote
    D.   an individual's personal decisions

Decision-Making

37.   Realists would base decision-making on
    A.   sound scientific procedures
    B.   experience and wisdom handed down from the past
    C.   natural instincts
    D.   personal convictions

38.   Thinking with a social conscience is an important element in the decision-making of
    A.   idealists
    B.   realists
    C.   pragmatists
    D.   existentialists

39.   Decision-making, according to idealists, should be based on
    A.   the laws which govern natural phenomena
    B.   commandments, constitutions, and traditions
    C.   democratic processes
    D.   one's thoughtful personal beliefs

40.   For an existentialist, good decisions are reached

A. through democratic processes
B. scientifically
C. by consulting authoritative sources
D. by relying on one's honest judgment while considering the consequences

Love

41.   As an example of what love means, and is, the idealist might cite
A.   maternal love
B.   serving one's fellow humans socially and politically
C.   caring for one's personal development
D.   performing selfless actions to conserve or protect nature

42.   For realists, love is probably best expressed by
A.   concern for one's fellow man
B.   care and concern for one's personal development
C.   respect for nature
D.   living up to the democratic ideal

43.   On the subject of love, existentialists would say that
A.   love is influenced by social learning, physical need, and emotional conditions
B.   knowing, understanding, and loving one's self is a prerequisite
C.   love is defined by and comes from God
D.   love is not a proper topic for investigation

44.   Serving others socially or politically would be an act of love for the
A.   existentialist
B.   pragmatist

C. realist
D. idealist

Future

45. With respect to the future, pragmatists tend to believe that
    A. it is in the hands of the individual
    B. it is preordained
    C. it can be, and is, influenced by humans interacting as social beings
    D. it is part of a closed system
46. In the philosophy of realism, the future resides in
    A. natural law and natural function
    B. the ability of human beings to interact wisely
    C. God's will
    D. the choices and actions of individual human beings
47. Idealists see the future as being
    A. governed by natural law and function
    B. part of a grand plan with a beginning and an end
    C. created as human beings interact in social environments
    D. in the hands of the individual
48. To an existentialist, the future is
    A. already determined
    B. controlled by natural law
    C. influenced by social events during the passage of time
    D. in the hands of the individual

Culture

49. Realists view culture as
     A. a part of nature to be learned and conserved by each new generation
     B. the collective thought and experience of human beings working together
     C. the creation of God
     D. a matter of personal meaning and relevance

50. The idea that culture and tradition are inseparable is consistent with the beliefs of
     A. existentialism
     B. pragmatism
     C. realism
     D. idealism

51. Culture, says the pragmatist, is
     A. developed as a result of society functioning according to laws of social and behavioral processes
     B. based on the absolutes of human existence
     C. created by humans as they use their intellect and communicate with each other
     D. an individual matter

52. According to existentialists, culture is determined by
     A. external forces and traditions
     B. individuals as they seek to understand themselves
     C. social processes and events
     D. scientific advances

Change

53. Innovations or technological advancements

which contradict the known or believed are
viewed with skepticism by
A. realists
B. idealists
C. existentialists
D. pragmatists

54. Change, to existentialists, is
A. determined by individuals as they make
personal decisions
B. determined by the laws of nature
C. determined by the leaders in a society
D. determined by fate

55. Pragmatists believe that change is
A. a slow process occurring in accordance with
nature's principles
B. a constant, ongoing, dynamic process
C. relevant only to the individual
D. a slow preordained process

56. Changes should be instigated only when they
are based on scientifically determined facts,
according to
A. idealists
B. realists
C. pragmatists
D. existentialists

Part II. The Four Philosophies
As They Apply to Educational Issues and Topics

57. In stating the purpose of education, pragmatists would probably stress the need for
    A. instruction in the classics
    B. experiences in democratic social processes
    C. instruction in the process of scientific investigation
    D. individual learning experiences

58. The overriding purpose of education according to existentialists is to
    A. educate the young in the laws, traditions, and beliefs of their culture
    B. prepare children to live harmoniously with nature
    C. help the young become fully authentic beings
    D. prepare children to live harmoniously with their fellow human beings

59. One would expect the curriculum of idealist schools to place emphasis on
    A. social studies
    B. fine arts
    C. the natural sciences and mathematics
    D. the liberal arts and humanities

60. In realist schools, the curriculum would probably be focused rather sharply on
    A. studies in the natural and behavioral sciences
    B. the humanities
    C. business and other practical subjects
    D. history and the fine arts

61. In addressing the subject matter of the curricu-

lum, pragmatist teachers would more than likely

A.   be highly structured
B.   rely heavily on the scientific method of inquiry
C.   exercise flexibility and try to be innovative
D.   encourage students to address it as they believe they should

62.   For the existentialist, that subject matter is important which is
A.   rooted in tradition
B.   personally meaningful
C.   related to natural law
D.   practical and useful

63.   The best sources of knowledge, says the idealist, are in
A.   nature and objective studies of natural phenomena
B.   accounts and observations of human events
C.   both of the above
D.   recognized histories and other authoritative documents handed down to us

64.   About knowledge, existentialists tend to believe that
A.   it is highly subjective
B.   it is relevant if it is useful
C.   it is finite
D.   it is most valid when it is acquired through objective, carefully controlled investigation

65.   The teacher who is a pragmatist sees himself/ herself mainly as a
A.   questioning and challenging presence
B.   motivating influence and facilitator
C.   leader whose role is to inspire

D.   knowledgeable authority

66.   High on the list of qualifications that a realist teacher would be expected to possess would be
A.   the ability to establish a friendly relationship with young people
B.   a broad sense of history
C.   good listening skills
D.   a sound understanding of scientific teaching techniques and methodology

67.   In a school where the philosophy of idealism prevails, play activities would likely be
A.   designed and disciplined by adults
B.   out-of-doors and, if possible, in natural surroundings
C.   oriented toward group cooperation
D.   unstructured

68.   In the view of existentialists, play should foster
A.   social development
B.   an appreciation of the natural order of things
C.   competitive art
D.   the development of the individual self

69.   Realist methods of instruction would emphasize
A.   recitation, memorization, and essay writing
B.   active participation in group activities
C.   words supported by pictures, diagrams, and things
D.   individual creative activities

70.   For instruction, pragmatist teachers tend to rely heavily on methods such as
A.   lecture and assigned reading and writing
B.   problem solving, role playing, and discussion
C.   field trips and research projects

D.   individual student expression and other elective activity

71.   The rules of an idealist school are likely to be based on
A.   democratic principles
B.   behavioral research
C.   tradition
D.   pupil-teacher dialogue

72.   It might be difficult to find a written set of rules in a school conducted by
A.   pragmatists
B.   existentialists
C.   idealists
D.   realists

73.   In schools where pragmatism is practiced, students would be expected to
A.   act like adults
B.   conform to school rules and social norms
C.   think freely and act responsibly
D.   exhibit curiosity and participate actively in the life of the school

74.   Realist teachers expect students to be
A.   organized in their study habits and orderly in their behavior
B.   cooperative, attentive, and respectful
C.   socially responsible
D.   individual decision makers

75.   Is teaching an art or a science? To that question, the idealist teacher would probably respond:
A.   It is very much a science.
B.   It is an irrelevant question.
C.   It is very much an art.
D.   It is both an art and a science.

76.   The existentialist teacher is most likely to view teaching as

A. the application of scientific methodology in a classroom

B. a personal encounter with a student

C. an interactive process that results in teacher-student learning

D. a performance that evokes student insight or learning

77. On the subject of individual student rights, idealists would probably argue that

A. children and adolescents in a democratic society must have freedom of choice and action

B. students should be strongly encouraged to experience life's variety of choices

C. equality under the law should prevail

D. children and adolescents are hardly capable of making significant life decisions

78. In existentialism, individual freedom is something that

A. should be extended to children

B. children know little about

C. should be encouraged about the time one enters high school

D. is better reserved for adulthood

79. Schools where students have a positive voice in governance and discipline matters would probably lean philosophically toward

A. idealism

B. realism

C. pragmatism

D. existentialism

80. Discipline procedures in realist schools would probably be characterized by

A. democratic principles

B. objectivity and consistency

C. permissiveness

D.   student self-governance
81.   Under fundamental idealist philosophy it is preferred that students assume the role of
A.   an active participant in group learning activities
B.   an attentive and respectful listener
C.   an independent learner
D.   a productive and responsible school citizen
82.   The existential teacher prefers students who are
A.   socially active and responsible
B.   obedient and scholarly
C.   sensitive and independently curious
D.   all of the above
83.   Pragmatist schools are most likely to address individual student differences by
A.   encouraging individual student research and creativity
B.   arranging group activities around individual interests, needs, and abilities
C.   tracking students into low, middle, and high ability groups
D.   individual tutoring
84.   The scientific measurement of human ability has been of great interest to
A.   idealists
B.   realists
C.   pragmatists
D.   existentialists
85.   In pragmatist schools, what is to be learned and how it will be accomplished are frequently derived from
A.   administrator-teacher decisions
B.   recommendations of specialists in the various fields of learning
C.   student interests

D.   teacher-pupil planning

86.   In establishing learning goals and objectives, realists prefer to rely on

A.   adults who are knowledgeable in the subject matter

B.   committees composed of parents, teachers, and students

C.   classical and traditional models of education

D.   dialogue between individual students and teachers

87.   For idealists, going back to the basics means not only renewed emphasis on the three R's but also on

A.   the natural and social sciences

B.   the humanities and the liberal arts

C.   consumer education and citizenship

D.   creative and performing arts

88.   The existentialist's return to the basics would include greater priority for

A.   problem-solving

B.   history and literature

C.   studies that are personally relevant

D.   computer science

89.   In testing student performance, realists place a lot of reliance on

A.   essay tests

B.   the application of principles

C.   guided self-evaluation

D.   objective and standardized tests

90.   An important purpose of testing in the pragmatist school is for

A.   diagnosing teacher effectiveness and student learning

B.   determining meritorious performance

    C. measuring a student's personal development

    D. separating the academically talented from the less talented

91. Properly inducting the young into the value structure of the parent society is a primary educational goal of

    A. pragmatists

    B. realists

    C. idealists

    D. existentialists

92. Existentialists believe that value education is best achieved
through

    A. teacher-guided experiences

    B. thoughtful, active involvement in decision-making

    C. reading great books

    D. studying nature

93. Pragmatists believe that a basic purpose of the school as a social institution is to

    A. bring culture to the young

    B. imitate society and life

    C. provide experiences that encourage the development of the self

    D. teach systematically that which is known

94. According to realists, the school serves an important social purpose because it

    A. teaches the importance of individual freedom

    B. nourishes the spiritual life of young people

    C. teaches young people how to adapt to their environment

    D. simulates life

95. Extracurricular activities in idealist schools

would probably be

    A. designed to meet the needs and interests of students

    B. strongly teacher-sponsor controlled

    C. dominated by sports

    D. informally organized by students

96. Adult supervision in school activities would probably be least in

    A. realist schools

    B. pragmatist schools

    C. existentialist schools

    D. idealist schools

97. School buildings designed by realist educators would probably feature

    A. lecture classrooms and libraries

    B. flexible space arrangements

    C. a variety of closed and open spaces

    D. labs and media centers

98. Physical arrangements in existentialist schools would encourage

    A. teacher-pupil dialogue and pupil creativity

    B. experiences in the manual and practical arts

    C. group interaction

    D. teacher-guided research

99. Words that appropriately describe the school climate preferred by pragmatists are

    A. studious and formal

    B. businesslike and orderly

    C. creative and reflective

    D. active and social

100. Realists want the climate of their schools to reflect

    A. efficiency and organization

    B. contemplation and inspiration

C.   practicality and social interaction

D.   openness and creativity

101.   If one were to look into an idealist classroom during the school day, the chances are good that the teacher would be

A.   moving about from small group to small group

B.   at the front of the room delivering a lecture

C.   carrying on a dialogue with a student

D.   at the head of the class instructing with some sort of visual aid

102.   Seating patterns in existential classrooms are often

A.   formal and fixed

B.   conducive to small group activity

C.   not discernible

D.   semicircular with a teacher station at front in the open area

103.   According to the pragmatist, a good way to provide leadership training in the American school is to

A.   nourish individual initiative

B.   require students to read the biographies of recognized leaders

C.   expect active student participation on committees and councils

D.   recognize the achievements of all who excel

104.   Leadership training in realist schools would probably be

A.   provided for those who ask for it

B.   focused on those who demonstrate the ability and inclination to lead

C.   provided through clubs and organizations

D.   none of the above

105.   For motivation, idealist teachers depend a lot on

    A.   their personality and ability to persuade
    B.   organization and reinforcement techniques
    C.   the active involvement of students in prob-lem-solving
    D.   the individual interests of their students

106.   In the opinion of existentialists, student motivation is best achieved by
    A.   encouraging students to participate in the social activities of the school
    B.   utilizing visual aids in the classroom
    C.   dynamic teacher performance
    D.   encouraging students to pursue their own interests

107.   Realists might define learning as
    A.   exercising and disciplining the mind
    B.   that which is relevant and meaningful to the self
    C.   a bonding of stimulus and response
    D.   the reconstruction of experience

108.   Important to learning, says the pragmatist, is
    A.   the learner's ability and willingness to read good books
    B.   the learner's involvement in problem-solving
    C.   the learner's sense of organization
    D.   the learner's creative ability

109.   The philosophy of idealism can be traced to such theorists as
    A.   Dewey and Lewin
    B.   Thorndike and Skinner
    C.   Plato and Saint Augustine
    D.   Rogers and Green

110.   The theory of insightful learning is highly regarded by
    A.   pragmatists

B.   existentialists

C.   idealists

D.   realists

111.   In defining teacher-administrator relations, realists tend to take their cue from

A.   military models

B.   business models

C.   democratic models

D.   a variety of models

112.   A key feature of teacher-administrator relations in pragmatist schools is

A.   "top down" communication

B.   organization

C.   interaction

D.   the "rap" session

113.   In the budget of an idealist school, priority would probably be given to

A.   the natural sciences

B.   the humanities

C.   social studies

D.   creative arts

114.   Where school funding is concerned, existentialists would probably place a relatively low priority on the

A.   social studies

B.   humanities

C.   natural sciences

D.   performing arts

115.   One of the following statements best describes realist thinking about creativity:

A.   External judgment of creativity is not important.

B.   Standards should be situational and flexible.

C. Creative effort should avoid anything radical.

D. Standards of creativity reside in nature and the mastery of technique.

116. Pragmatists would probably discourage creative efforts that are

A. imitative

B. inventive

C. utilitarian

D. not personally inspired

117. The role of a counselor in an idealist school would probably be similar to that of

A. guidance worker

B. non-directive listener and reflector

C. diagnostician of personal and social problems

D. mentor or dean

118. The purpose of counseling in an existential school is to

A. help students discover meaning in their personal life

B. help students solve personal and social problems

C. compile data on students and recommend appropriate courses of action based on the data

D. turn young people into the adults they ought to be

119. Illustrated textbooks were first introduced by

A. idealists

B. realists

C. pragmatists

D. existentialists

120. The pragmatist would strongly suggest that textbooks should be supplemented with

A. well-delivered lectures
B. independent research
C. direct or vicarious experience
D. recitation

121. On the subject of modern humanism, idealists would probably take the position that it (modern humanism)
A. leads to the erosion of moral fiber
B. is acceptable as long as it contributes to the improvement of the individual and society
C. dilutes the rigor of the traditional curriculum
D. both A and C

122. Existential thought and modern humanism are
A. not comparable
B. incompatible
C. fully compatible
D. compatible to some extent

123. Two educational theorists whom pragmatists hold in high regard are
A. A. S. Neill and Maxine Greene
B. W. H. Kilpatrick and Boyd Bode
C. Herbert Spencer and J. F. Broudy
D. Herman Horne and W. T. Harris

124. Behavioral psychology is associated most closely with the philosophy of
A. existentialism
B. idealism
C. realism
D. pragmatism

125. Material dealing with vocational and career education would be a very important part of the collection in the library of a/an
A. realist school
B. existentialist school

    C. pragmatist school

    D. idealist school

126. The attitude of realists toward the use of technology in the classroom would probably be

    A. indifferent

    B. positive

    C. negative

    D. much like the attitude of idealists

Answer key for the Review Test

1. B	26. B	51. C	76. B	101. B
2. C	27. C	52. B	77. D	102. C
3. A	28. C	53. B	78. A	103. C
4. B	29. D	54. A	79. C	104. B
5. C	30. D	55. B	80. B	105. A
6. D	31. B	56. B	81. B	106. D
7. C	32. C	57. B	82. C	107. C
8. A	33. D	58. C	83. B	108. B
9. D	34. A	59. D	84. B	109. C
10. B	35. B	60. A	85. D	110. B
11. A	36. B	61. C	86. A	111. B
12. D	37. A	62. B	87. B	112. C
13. C	38. C	63. D	88. C	113. B
14. B	39. B	64. A	89. D	114. C
15. B	40. D	65. B	90. A	115. D
16. A	41. A	66. D	91. C	116. A
17. B	42. C	67. A	92. B	117. D
18. D	43. B	68. D	93. B	118. A
19. C	44. B	69. C	94. C	119. B
20. A	45. C	70. B	95. B	120. C
21. C	46. A	71. C	96. C	121. D
22. A	47. B	72. B	97. D	122. D
23. B	48. D	73. D	98. A	123. B
24. C	49. A	74. A	99. D	124. C
25. D	50. D	75. C	100. A	125. C
				126. B

Glossary

Absolute.   Describes that which is unchanging, total, timeless, or perfect (as in *truth*).

Aesthetics.   The branch of philosophy which deals with art, creativity, and beauty.

Affective.   Relating to attitudes, emotions, interests, and preferences. The emotive side of human character as opposed to the cognitive side.

Agnosticism.   A position holding that it is impossible for humans to attain real knowledge of God.

Altruism.   Behavior promoting the welfare of others. Other-oriented actions performed out of love, benevolence, or unselfish concern.

A posteriori.   Knowledge gained through direct human experience. A posteriori reasoning begins with experience and infers conclusions (inductive).

A priori.   Knowledge which can be gained through reason alone. A priori reasoning is either (1) the acceptance of predetermined universal and necessarily valid knowledge, or (2) the use of a logic system without requiring observation or external testing (deductive).

Atheism.   Not theistic. Not believing in a supreme being. The rejection of the notion of the existence of divine super force.

Authenticity.   Quality of genuiness. The development of the truest self and the fulfillment of the greatest personal potential (without conformity ungenuineness).

Anthropomorphism.   The attribution of human characteristics to divine or all-powerful forces controlling the universe, society, and human effort.

Axiology.   The study of the theory of value. The investigation into goodness or what man "ought" to do.

Becoming.   Fulfilling or actualizing one's personal potential. Implies an ongoing process—"ing."

Behaviorism.   A school of psychology restricted to the study of behavior itself without reference to mind, mental processes, consciousness, or emotions.

Categorical imperative.   The supreme moral law governing human behavior (idealism).

Chauvinism.   Excessive and blindly held patriotism. Unreasoning devotion to one's own nation, race, sex, tribe and contempt for all others.

Cognitive.   Relating to information, facts, knowledge, the intellectual side of human character as opposed to the affective or emotive side.

Coherence theory of truth.   Determines truth or validity based upon the degree to which data from a variety of sources cohere or stick together logically with propositions or ideas already present in the mind.

Compensatory education. Educational strategies designed to remove social, economic, and/or educational barriers caused by poverty, cultural milieu, or institutional racism.

Conditioning. The association of stimulus and response and reinforcement in a pattern which increases the likelihood of the strengthening of the response upon the perception of the stimulus on subsequent occasions.

Correspondence theory of truth. A theory of truth which uses as the test the existence of direct exact relationship (one-to-one) between the elements of a fact and the proposition which is alleged to describe or govern that fact.

Creationism. Belief which rejects the scientific and evolutionary theory of the origin of the universe in favor of the idea of divine creation by a super force, namely God.

Critical realism. A perspective which affirms that the world is independent of human perception or conception of it and that humans cannot perceive or know it directly. Humans can know it only through (psychological) perceptual filters which may (or may not) distort our ability to "see" the world clearly.

Cultural pluralism. Promotes the idea that an overall society (the U.S.A.) is a collection of cultural and ethnic groups each having its own rituals, values, folkways, and mores and each one entitled to be sustained rather than submerged into a single "melting pot" culture.

Cynicism. The attribute of questioning the sincerity and goodness of people. Sometimes extended to doubting the "truth" told by others.

Deductive method. A problem-solution methodology in which conclusions follow from an accepted pre-

mise (or premises). It begins with knowledge which
is accepted or believed to be truth. All conclusions
follow logically from those premises.

Deschooling. Founded on the belief that modern
societies have become so "institutionalized" as to be
hindrances and barriers to the people they allege to
be helping. Modern society has lost both the individual's ability to control his or her own purpose and
control the milieu within which humans function.
School must be radicallly changed, de-institutional-
ized, and disestablished.

Determinism. The philosophic position that law
(natural, physical, universal) governs every fact and
action. Everything has a cause and the causes are
the key to understanding. It embraces the concept
that in human behavior there is no such thing as free
will or free choice.

Dialectic. Pertaining to the art of reasoning and discussion as in debate.

Dualism. The controlling presence of two factors
(good-evil, mind-body, rational-irrational) which may
lead to conflict or a hierarchy of dominance.

Eclecticism. The building of a philosophy by drawing
elements from various philosophies. It requires that
the elements be selected with care and deliberation
and be fitted into an intellectually integrated system
with no conflicts. It is neither an unconscious selection of a hodgepodge of ideas nor a whimsically
created "house of cards."

Empiricism. The sole source of knowledge is experience. Denies use of a priori knowledge and any
innate knowledge. Sometimes inappropriately used
as a synonym for pragmatism.

Epistemology. The study of knowledge—its structure,
validity, origins, and methods or tests.

Essence. The characteristics of a thing viewed independently of its existence. The attempt to describe by listing what it is like.

Essentialism. An educational reaction to progressive trends in the first quarter of the 20th century. It was reactionary in intent and advocated a body of "essential" curriculum (the basics) and focused on method, content, and management rather than creative thinking, relevance, or innovation. Feared the loss of democracy and discipline and the dilution of standards and morals. W. C. Bagley.

Ethics. The study of rightness and wrongness, goodness and badness. The rules of correct conduct.

Ethnocentrism. The belief that one's own culture, nation, values, rituals, and goals are naturally and automatically superior to those of any other nation or group.

Existence. Things accepted for their existing without prior consideration of their characteristics or essences.

Existential moment. The point in individuals' existences when they realize and recognize their aloneness and their alienation from other human beings. The recognition of unique individuality, responsibility and ultimate freedom along with possible dread, fear, and despair.

Experimentalism. Based on the use of experimental methodology of the sciences (hypothesis, data collection, testing, conclusions). Sometimes used as a synonym for pragmatism.

Field theory. The psychological perspective which attempts to organize perception along the lines of fields of force in physics. The meaning of an event is determined by the environment (total field) at that time. Present events are interrelated with all influences (past, present, or future) that determine behavior.

Free will.   Unlike determinism, the doctrine of free will assumes the human being to have freedom of choice and action.

Gestalt psychology.   Psychology based upon the perceived, organized whole. The parts derive their character from the whole. The whole is greater than the sum of the parts.

Hedonism.   Human motivation considered to be based on seeking pleasure and avoiding pain.

Humanism.   Philosophic perspective in which the welfare and happiness of mankind is paramount. A philosophical and educational creed emphasizing the importance of the human being and human values as opposed to religious orthodoxy or abstractions. The individual is viewed as an autonomous reasoning being whose own intellect is the ultimate test of truth. Educationally, it opposes schools which are psychologically destructive or academically impotent. It opposes both the lock-step approach of the traditional school and the mechanism of trendy behaviorism.

Humanities.   The human history subjects in the studies of the liberal arts curriculum: literature, art, philosophy, religion, and intellectual history.

Inductive reasoning.   Generalizations based upon observation and experience. Conclusions are summative but do not exceed the limits of observed data.

Innate.   Inborn information, ideas, facts. Ideas which all humans possess at birth.

Instrumentalism.   Use of the mind as an instrument to construct truth from experiences. Early name for pragmatism.

Intuition.   Knowledge based not upon experience or

reason but upon its sudden appearance in the mind. Comprehension without reason or experience.

Learning. A change in behavior occurring as a result of experiences in the life of the learner. Learning is inferred from performance and also from the conditions existing at or before the occurrence of the "learning."

Logic (formal). The study of deductive reasoning as a method.

Logic (general). Any system approach to determining the validity of an idea.

Materialism. Devotion to and seeking of material goods or wealth rather than spiritual values.

Metaphysics. The study of being and the study of what is real.

Naive realism. The unsophisticated perspective which believes that human beings can really know the external (real) world and that all knowledge is in the external world.

Naturalism. Philosophy that the external physical world needs no supernatural cause or control but is a self-sufficient system and can be understood as such.

Neo-Thomism. The prevailing philosophy of the church based on elements of traditional idealism and realism which were combined through the efforts of St. Thomas Aquinas. Uses the syllogism in Aristotelian logic and defends Christian humanism.

Nihilism. The belief that nothing exists or is knowable. Seeks progress through destruction (anarchy) and denies moral principles or social obligations.

Ontology. The study and theory of being.

Original sin. Traced to Adam and Eve in the Old Testament of the Bible. With eating the apple (fruit of the tree of knowledge) subsequent generations were condemned to damnation and to seek salvation through prayer, acceptance of Christ, obedience and service to the church.

Orthodoxy. Beliefs which are declared by a power group to be paramount. Belief contrary to an orthodox position is heresy.

Paradox. A set of circumstances which are simultaneously true and false. Something self-contradictory. A concept containing the elements of both truth and falsity.

Pedagogy. An early name for the science and study of teaching. A school teacher is a pedagogue.

Phenomenology. Based on the notion that knowledge is limited to physical and mental phenomena. The mind performs an analysis of mental processes which are subjective and conscious. It is closely associated with existentialism.

Premise. A statement of belief or accepted truth from which an inference is drawn in deductive (syllogistic) reasoning.

Process. Ongoing series of movements, thoughts or actions reaching toward progress, change, growth, or destruction. Usually considered to have purpose and direction.

Progressive education. Attempted in the first quarter of the 20th century to meet needs of an (1) ideal society and (2) individualism through involvement of the whole child in an experience-oriented curriculum in a school setting which is child-centered rather than subject-centered.

Quadrivium. Proposed originally by Plato as the advanced portion of liberal arts: arithmetic, geometry, astronomy, and music. Used in the medieval period as the curriculum.

Reconstructionism. Belief in the use of philosophy and education to cause the reconstruction and improvement of human society, culture, law and government (Theodore Brameld).

Relativism. Generally a rejection of absolutes and an acceptance of the idea of the ever-changing nature of the universe, especially in regard to time and environment.

Scholasticism. Typical philosophy of emerging Christianity in its early centuries believing that philosophic thought is subordinate to theology.

Semantics. Study of the relationships of words (symbols) to each other and to the concepts, events, or objects which they represent. The study of meaning in language.

Situational ethics. The concept that the rules of right behavior are relative and not fixed and that those rules are dependent upon time, place, and circumstance.

Skepticism. Idea that no knowledge or no verifiable knowledge of the absolute or the perfect is possible. Doubting and questioning the validity of information offered as Truth.

Social science. Branches of science concerned with human events, history, and interaction. Each branch applies direct observation and scientific methods to investigate its specific areas of interest. Sociology, anthropology, economics, political science, geography, history.

Social studies. Social studies is an organization of public school curriculum around issues and questions of relevance in today's world in which the narrow boundaries of each of the social sciences must be bridged as knowledge from several social sciences may be utilized in answering the questions and solving the problems around which the curriculum is organized.

Socratic method.   A teaching method in which through skillfully systematic questioning the teacher draws forth increasingly more complex ideas and answers from the student. The teacher claims not to be teaching new knowledge but drawing forth ideas innately imbedded in the mind of the student. Generally, a teaching technique using teacher questioning to cause the learner to reach new (higher) conclusions.

Subjective knowledge.   The idea that all knowledge perceived by the individual is judged, created, or constructed by the individual perceiver.

Superforce.   Synonym for any of the all-powerful forces which cause and direct the actions of the universe, society, and human beings. Examples would include God, Jehovah, Allah, the cycle of history, or the all-powerful political state, nationalism, and theocracies.

Syllogism.   A reasoning (logic) device using two premises (or previously accepted truths) to reach a conclusion.

Teleology.   The idea that there are goals, purposes, ultimate ends, and so on. Teleology explains the past and the present by references to the future and to final causes and values rather than trying to explain the contemporary and future situations by reference to the past.

Transcendentalism.   Belief in knowledge beyond the senses or beyond experience. It is concerned with a priori knowledge. Idealistic thought advocates the imminent presence of the ideal or spiritual. Transcendentalism is based on reasoning and intuition rather than empirical data.

Trivium.   The first three subjects in the medieval education called the seven liberal arts—grammar, rhetoric, and dialectic. Originated in Plato's *Republic III*. (See also quadrivium.)

Utilitarianism.   Idea that an act is good or right if it results in the greatest utility and pleasure for the world. If it works, it is good or useful.

Utopia.   The ideal state. Imaginary states have been conceived by several philosophers and attempted by several social reformers.

Bibliography

Idealism

Barrett, Clifford, *Contemporary Idealism in America*, New York, Macmillan Company, 1932.

Bogoslovsky, B. B., *The Ideal School*, New York, Macmillan Company, 1936.

Butler, J. Donald, *Idealism in Education*, New York, Harper & Row, 1966.

Donohue, John W., S. J., *Catholicism and Education*, New York, Harper and Row, 1973.

Gentile, Giovanni, *The Reform of Education*, New York, Harcourt, Brace & World, 1922.

Horne, Herman H., *Idealism in Education*, New York, Macmillan Company, 1910.

Horne, Herman Harrell, *The Philosophy of Christian Education*, New York, Fleming H. Revell Company, 1937.

Realism

Breed, Frederick, S., *Education and the New Realism*, New York, Macmillan, 1939.
Broudy, Harry S., *Building a Philosophy of Education*, Englewood Cliffs, New Jersey, Prentice Hall, 1961.
Herbert, J. F., *The Science of Education*, Boston, D.C. Heath, 1983.
Locke, John, *Some Thoughts Concerning Education*, Cambridge, England. At the University Press, 1934.
Perry, Ralph Barton, *Realms of Value*, Cambridge, Harvard University Press, 1954.
Martin, W. O., *Realism in Education*, New York, Harper and Row, 1966.
Whitehead, A. N., *The Aims of Education*, New York, Macmillan, 1929.
Wild, John, *Introduction to Realist Philosophy*, New York, Harper, 1948.

Pragmatism

Bayles, Ernest E., *Pragmatism and Education*, New York, Harper and Row, 1966.
Bode, Boyd H., *Modern Education Theories*, New York, Macmillan, 1927.
Childs, John L., *American Pragmatism and Education*, New York, Holt, Rinehart and Winston, 1956.
Dewey, John, *Democracy and Education*, New York, Macmillan, 1916.
Dewey, John, *Experience as Education*, New York, Macmillan, 1938.

Dworkin, Martin S. (Ed.), *Dewey on Education*, New York, Teachers College Press, 1959.

Hook, Sidney, *Education and Modern Man*, New York, Alfred A. Knopf, 1963.

Horne, H. H., *The Democratic Philosophy of Education*, New York, Macmillan, 1932.

James, William, *Talks to Teachers*, New York, Holt, Rinehart and Winston, 1946.

James, William, *Pragmatism*, New York, Green & Co., 1907.

Kilpatrick, W. H., *Philosophy of Education*, New York, Macmillan, 1963.

Existentialism

Barrett, William, *Irrational Man*, New York, Doubleday & Company, 1953.

Buber, Martin, *I and Thou*, New York, Scribner's, 1970.

Greene, Maxine, (ed.), *Existential Encounters for Teachers*, New York, Random House, 1967.

Green, Maxine, *Teacher as Stranger*, Belmont, California, Wadsworth, 1973.

Kneller, George F., *Existentialism in Education*, New York, John Wiley & Sons, 1964.

Lesnoff-Caravagla, Gari, *Education as Existential Possibility*, New York, Philosophical Library, 1972.

Morris, VanCleve, *Existentialism in Education*, New York, Harper and Row, 1966.

Neill, A. S., *Summerhill—A Radical Approach to Child Rearing*, New York, Hart, 1960.

General Resources

Brubacher, John S., *Modern Philosophies of Education*, New York, McGraw-Hill, 1939.

Butler, J. Donald, *Four Philosophies and Their Practice in Education and Religion*, New York, Harper nd Row, 1968.

Kneller, G. F., *Foundations of Education*, John Wiley & Sons, 1963.

Morris, Van Cleve, and Pai, Young, *Philosophy and the American School*, Boston, Houghton Mifflin, 1976.

Phenix, P. H. (ed.), *Philosophies of Education*, New York, John Wiley and Sons, 1961.

Strain, John Paul, *Modern Philosophies of Education*, New York, Random House, 1971.